EFT for CHRISTIANS

Tap for Jesus!

Sherrie Rice Smith

by Sherrie Rice Smith

www.EFTUniverse.com

Energy Psychology Press
3340 Fulton Rd, #442, Fulton, CA 95439
www.energypsychologypress.com

Cataloging-in-Publication Data

EFT for christians / by Sherrie Rice Smith
    p. cm.
Includes bibliographical references and index.
ISBN 978-1-60415-251-7
1. Christianity—Psychology. 1. Psychology and religion. I. Title.
BR1702.155 2015
261.5'15—dc22

All scripture verses used in this book are from the New International Version (NIV); see References at the end of the book for other translations utilized.

Scriptural advisor and Consultant: Rev. Paul Borgman, MDiv, STM, DMin
Book research: Carol Helberg Wallis
Manuscript development/editing:
S. A. "Sam" Jernigan (Renaissance Consultations)
Cover design by Victoria Valentine
Editing by Stephanie Marohn
Typesetting by Karin Kinsey
Typeset in Cochin and Adobe Garamond
Printed in USA by Bang Printing
10 9 8 7 6 5 4 3 2 1

Important note: While EFT (Emotional Freedom Techniques) has produced remarkable clinical results, it must still be considered to be in the experimental stage and thus practitioners and the public must take complete responsibility for their use of it. Further, Sherrie Rice Smith and Dawson Church (the authors) are not licensed mental health professionals and they offer the information in this book solely as life coaches. Readers are strongly cautioned and advised to consult with a physician, psychologist, psychiatrist, or other licensed health care professional before utilizing any of the information in this book. The information is based on information from sources believed to be accurate and reliable and every reasonable effort has been made to make the information as complete and accurate as possible, but such completeness and accuracy cannot be guaranteed and is not guaranteed.

The author, publisher, and contributors to this book, and their successors, assigns, licensees, employees, officers, directors, attorneys, agents, and other parties related to them (a) do not make any representations, warranties, or guarantees that any of the information will produce any particular medical, psychological, physical, or emotional result; (b) are not engaged in the rendering of medical, psychological or other advice or services; (c) do not provide diagnosis, care, treatment, or rehabilitation of any individual; and (d) do not necessarily share the views and opinions expressed in the information. The information has not undergone evaluation and testing by the United States Food and Drug Administration or similar agency of any other country and is not intended to diagnose, treat, prevent, mitigate, or cure any disease. Risks that might be determined by such testing are unknown. If the reader purchases any services or products as a result of the information, the reader or user acknowledges that the reader or user has done so with informed consent. The information is provided on an "as is" basis without any warranties of any kind, express or implied, whether warranties as to use, merchantability, fitness for a particular purpose, or otherwise.

The author, publisher, and contributors to this book, and their successors, assigns, licensees, employees, officers, directors, attorneys, agents, and other parties related to them (a) expressly disclaim any liability for and shall not be liable for any loss or damage including but not limited to use of the information; (b) shall not be liable for any direct or indirect compensatory, special, incidental, or consequential damages or costs of any kind or character; (c) shall not be responsible for any acts or omissions by any party including but not limited to any party mentioned or included in the information or otherwise; (d) do not endorse or support any material or information from any party mentioned or included in the information or otherwise; and (e) will not be liable for damages or costs resulting from any claim whatsoever. The within limitation of warranties may be limited by the laws of certain states and/or other jurisdictions and so some of the foregoing limitations may not apply to the reader who may have other rights that vary from state to state. If the reader or user does not agree with any of the terms of the foregoing, the reader or user should not use the information in this book or read it. A reader who continues reading this book will be deemed to have accepted the provisions of this disclaimer.

Please consult qualified health practitioners regarding your use of EFT.

Contents

Foreword

Jesus is often called "the great physician" because of the many healing miracles attributed to him. The Gospel of Saint Matthew 12:14, one of many such texts, tells us that the blind and lame came to Jesus in the Temple, and that he healed them. Healing has been part of the Christian faith since its humble beginnings, with accounts of healing by Jesus's disciples, and then a great many by the mystics and saints that followed them in subsequent generations.

I have been privileged to meet several noted contemporary Christian healers, such as Francis MacNutt. Rev. MacNutt is a former Dominican priest and author of the classic book *Healing*, which has sold close to half a million copies (MacNutt, 1977). He has traveled all over the world offering healing prayer, sometimes to groups of thousands of people, and there are hundreds of accounts of miraculous healing attributed to his ministry. In his book *The Healing Reawakening* (MacNutt, 2006), he reviews the history of the early Church, and argues that the many miraculous healings that occurred in that period led directly to Christianity becoming the official faith of the Roman Empire.

Another priest, Rev. Ron Roth, was featured in a book called *Soul Medicine* that I coauthored with Harvard-trained neurosurgeon Norman Shealy, MD, PhD (Shealy & Church, 2007). From among the hundreds of grateful letters written to him with accounts of healing, we were able to find three cases in which a medically diagnosed disease had been verifiably healed. The Christian tradition of healing is alive and well.

One of the central problems presented by modernity is the relationship of medical breakthroughs to faith-based healing. Some sects completely reject contemporary medicine and place their faith entirely in prayer. A case that made headlines was that of Ashley King, who died at the age of 12 in 1988. Her parents, both Christian Scientists, had rejected conventional medicine for the treatment of a large tumor on her right leg. She received only non-medical care in a Christian Science nursing home, in which she allegedly did not even receive pain medication, and died in extreme pain. The parents were charged with child abuse.

The vast majority of Christians, of whatever persuasion, perceive little or no conflict between modern medicine and faith-based healing. We don't usually reject getting antibiotics for a bacterial infection, or surgery for a torn ligament, on the basis of faith. We don't reject psychotherapy when we're anxious or depressed.

Instead, we avail ourselves of the best of modern medicine, and we also pray. Few Christians perceive any conflict between one and the other. Indeed, there is good evidence from science that prayer enhances healing (Dossey, 2000). Rev. MacNutt is also the cofounder of the Christian Therapy Association, and there are many religious psychotherapists who combine prayer with evidence-based psychotherapeutic methods like cognitive behavioral therapy, acceptance and commitment therapy, exposure therapy, interpersonal therapy, and family psychoeducation.

One such evidence-based technique, EFT or Emotional Freedom Techniques, has spread quickly to become, in the words of an article on Examiner.com, "one of the most successful psychology self-help techniques ever developed" (Russell, 2014). EFT uses elements of exposure and cognitive therapies, and combines them with acupressure (fingertip pressure on acupuncture points). Human trials using fMRI technology have shown that acupuncture regulates the parts of the brain that process the fear response (Hui et al., 2005; Fang et al., 2009; Napadow et al., 2007). Combining acupressure with proven techniques from psychotherapy usually produces much quicker treatment time frames, as well as better outcomes for clients, than psychotherapy alone (Church, Feinstein, Palmer-Hoffman, Stein, & Tranguch, 2014).

In this book, Sherrie Rice Smith does us the valuable service of explaining how we can use new healing methods like EFT in the context of Christian faith. Just as—in addition to prayer and supplication—we embrace psychotherapy for mental illness, and medicine for physical disease, we have access to a wide array of conventional and alternative approaches to support our health.

She begins by outlining the marvelous biochemical and neurological processes through which our bodies function, and the role of hormones like cortisol and DHEA and neurotransmitters like serotonin and dopamine in regulating the stress response.

She then squarely addresses various common misperceptions, such as that because EFT isn't found in the Bible it is not part of God's pharmacopeia of healing methods. Neither are aspirin or CAT scans! She laces her arguments with powerful stories drawn from her Christian EFT practice, showing how faith and EFT combine to produce profound psychological shifts, and in some cases physical healing as well.

I found some of these particularly moving. My father was a missionary evangelist, and most of my extended family includes clergy and lay ministers. I've watched some family members struggling with difficult life issues from addiction to marital infidelity to foreclosure, and trying to resolve them by faith alone, not availing themselves of some of the practical secular tools that research shows to be effective. They usually failed, and entered into a vicious psychological cycle of recrimination and self-blame, fueled by the guilt that afflicts so many Christians. Sherrie tells the story of how she and her family found themselves in a similar downward spiral for many years, until she discovered EFT.

You'll be inspired by how practical and engaging Sherrie's advice is, and how effectively she moves from theology to psychology to physiology and back. You'll also sense immediately how passionately she cares about healing—yours, mine, hers—and how urgent her message is that breakthroughs in wellness are possible as we embrace all the healing options with which the Creator has endowed us. Sherrie's approach of engaging common-sense healing methods with faith-based practices offers us the best of both worlds, and a pathway to success that unites faith and science.

—Dawson Church, PhD

Acknowledgments

I would like to thank a few people for helping to save my life, literally. First and foremost, to my Lord and Savior, Jesus Christ, who has stood by me through thick and thin, kept me safe from my suicidal thoughts multiple times, thus allowing me to learn the difficult lessons of life. I praise Him for delivering me to this appointed place He wanted me to be in establishing a version of Emotional Freedom Techniques (EFT) that would be acceptable to Christians worldwide. My sole desire is to serve Him every minute of every day, my will totally surrendered to His, in whatever capacity He has for me—and I'm so blessed to be directly involved in delivering a method of deep healing for His people.

To my husband, Brad, who has put up with my journey, one unlike anything he has ever seen, I love you, honey, and I thank you.

In no particular order, next are my friends, some for decades, some newer, but all of them important to my journey. To Carol Helberg Wallis, who prayed me out of more scrapes than I probably ever realized and who did an immense amount of background research work for this book—thank you. To the Rev. Dr. Paul and Pat Borgman—I am extremely grateful to Paul for undertaking the first book edit and checking my theology and doctrine—you are the greatest! To Joan Emery and Susan Marshall, to my neighbors Kathy Schultz and Kathy Dorlack, to my dear Aunt Jeanne Paff, and to Joan Todd, all of whom have listened patiently as I told and retold the stories of my childhood, trying to find a way to digest them, to heal them, pre-EFT, and to cleanse myself of the internal agony embedded in hate, anger, resentment, shame, humiliation, embarrassment, confusion, fear, worry, unworthiness, remorse, sadness, frustration, inadequacy, betrayal, disappointment, and a hundred more burdensome emotions. To Judy Wiedenkeller, my "older" sister in Christ, who unbeknownst to her, has mentored me along, lovingly answering crazy life questions without prejudice, also just permitting me to be me as we travel along this life's trail in our shared Christian faith. To Dee Whitaker and Leny Chrisman, both of whom just "found" me and my Christian EFT website on the Internet. They have each been a source of encouragement to me as this book has progressed. To Melinda Utal-Martinez—what fun we have had discussing all things EFT via e-mails, I so appreciate your encouragement. A big thank-you to Kim Eisen, EFT-INT, in Minneapolis, who tapped with Brad, discharging his hate for his abusive, now-deceased parents—you are always there for us! To Marion Allen who understood me from day one and who has encouraged me to keep on plodding the EFT highway wherever God so leads. To Valerie Lis who mentored me along the EFT way, and to Alina Frank who has permitted me to ask countless questions that she patiently answered quickly and kindly. To S. A. "Sam" Jernigan, a great big Thank You for contributing your invaluable organizational and writing skills to this book's development, as well as for proving to be a trusted navigator (and advocate) for me in these unfamiliar new author waters.

And, finally, to Dawson Church, I give a big hug and heartfelt thank-you for introducing me to EFT and for giving me this opportunity to bring a Christian perspective to the EFT community. My lengthy professional background in nursing and decades-long relationship with Jesus have caused this to feel like a heaven-sent mission indeed, and I'm truly grateful for your accommodation as well as encouragement.

To anyone else I inadvertently missed, it was not purposeful. My heart overflows with gratitude to each and every one of you for the gifts you've bestowed on me. I couldn't have done it without you! I love you all from the bottom of my now-overflowing heart, the one that was stone-cold and dead before I discovered the transformative power of EFT.

1

A Personal EFT Beginning

Three years ago, I didn't care if I was dead or alive. I had tried all kinds of conventional therapies, drugs, and advice from friends and pastors—all to no avail. My life was plainly out of control.

At the height of his legal career, my younger brother, Bill, had just died of ALL (leukemia) at age 47, leaving behind a wife and four daughters under the age of 20. As his oldest sister and a registered nurse, I participated in much of Bill's disease process, traveling between Wisconsin, Pennsylvania, and New York several times. My husband, Brad, and I drove 2,500 miles to attend two wakes for him at opposite ends of the state of Pennsylvania, ending back in our hometown to bury him in the family plot.

While Brad was wonderful throughout this long ordeal, allowing me to do what I needed to do for my brother, he had his own issues, and we simply were not getting along at all. Grief set in, as I expected it to, and

I felt as though I were headed, once again, for another depression. My immediate family dynamics seemed to disintegrate during Bill's 2-year bout with cancer. The leukemia had gotten Bill, and it appeared to be taking me under too.

Turmoil in my life, a drastic diet I undertook, a dying brother, the traumatic death of my sister Karen at 17 months of age, a rocky marriage—these are small pieces of my background. Let me set the stage a bit here.

I was raised in a staunch Roman Catholic family, attended parochial school for 8 years and then public high school (only because a Catholic high school was no longer convenient), followed by Catholic nursing school, St. Vincent's Hospital School of Nursing, in Erie, Pennsylvania.

Sometime during high school, I began questioning what the nuns had taught us about our Catholic faith. There was no one I felt comfortable asking about it all. We were always told to "just believe." I muddled my way through, doing what I could to figure out these weighty spiritual matters on my own. I remember buying my first Bible while in Erie. A nagging of sorts prompted me to make that purchase; now I understand it was the Holy Spirit leading me in my desire to know more of the Lord. I had an abbreviated copy of Psalms that I'd read as a teenager, but I had never owned a real Bible.

Nursing school was no picnic for me emotionally. I gained a lot of weight in the first 3 or 4 months of my freshman year. I didn't date at all because I was scared to death of men. Looking back, I suspect I didn't date because of all the weight I had gained. Something was seriously amiss.

In my second year of nursing school, during my pediatrics rotation, I experienced my first depression. Everything seemed to crash in on me. Medications stabilized me, however, and somehow I graduated nursing school as a registered nurse.

After completing my education, I returned to the small western Pennsylvania town where I had grown up. I lived at home, worked part time at the local hospital time (the only job available) while working for my dad in the family business for 6 months until the job I desired opened up at Frontier Nursing Service (FNS).

When I accepted that job, Mom asked me, "Are you still thinking about doing that?" I was, and I did. I left for FNS on January 4, 1974.

I wasn't old enough to drink in the state of Pennsylvania, but I was off on an adventure of a lifetime in the mountains of southeastern Kentucky where, until the late 1960s, RNs were still riding horses up into "those hollers" to visit the sick and deliver babies in the homes of the mountain residents. By 1974, four-wheel-drive jeeps were the mode of transportation and off I went to try my hand at remote mountain nursing. This was such a huge turning point in my life because I had matured emotionally, professionally, and spiritually that I began telling everyone I grew up in Kentucky.

The nursing activities I performed still send chills up my spine — I was only 20 years old, but what responsibility I was given! Someone saw some abilities in me because

I tended to be the one tagged when something odd or unusual needed doing. It all should have frightened me, like the night a woman arrived in the emergency room after accidentally drinking a glass of Clorox, or the day an 18-month baby boy died in my arms while we transported him in a Volkswagen 30 miles over the mountains to a larger medical facility. I was simply too young to know I should be scared!

During this period in Kentucky, I had lots of time to think. Lots of emotional stuff surfaced as a result. As we RNs ate our meals communally, all 75 of us, we typically discussed medicine, nursing, and religion. As I interacted with those women of all different faith backgrounds, God used various women there to answer all those questions that had popped up for me in high school.

Slowly, Jesus drew me closer to Him. We only attended Mass every third weekend when a priest came to town. One beautiful day in April 1975, with redbud and white dogwood blooming among pines in the surrounding woods, I gave my life to Jesus in St. Christopher's Chapel. I'll never forget the intense inner peace I felt in that surrender. My life course was now up to Him. He could use me as He wished for His own purposes. I had no idea of the ride that was about to begin!

Life went on for the next 30 or 40 years. Jobs, job changes, relocations, new churches, and marriage ensued. All the while the emotional turmoil from my youth and early life lived on in my heart and mind. That never seemed to change. Upsetting and unsettling memories were just plain stuck inside me, and they only worsened as the years progressed.

I tried counseling and using emotional release methods I read about in magazines and books, but nothing held. I couldn't shake loose the private traumas. I tried it all. Nothing worked. My emotional pain continued unabated.

When my brother died, life just seemed to be at its worst for me. How much more could I endure? God had a plan, however, and what a plan it was!

The autumn after Bill's death, I lay on the living room carpet, crying and praying, wrestling with God. Over and over, He asked me, "Are you now ready to give it ALL to me this time?"

Sadly, over the years, as many Christians do, I had taken back control of various aspects of my life. I guess I figured I could handle them better than God! Wrestling was a good word for this struggle and it went on for 3 days. I felt like Jacob wrestling with the angel. Every time I started to answer God, "Yes," I couldn't get the word out of my mouth. Finally, my resistance gave way and I gave in—again. Thirty-five years after that first surrender to my Savior, I re-surrendered my life completely to Jesus that day.

Within 3 days, Colleen Lantzy, a behavioral psychologist acquaintance, phoned me inquiring after my health. Well, frankly, I was feeling horrible, and I admitted this to her. Oh, I know God had His hand on me and I would get through it all—I always did—but it just wasn't much fun and I was struggling as a result.

Colleen asked if I knew about EFT. "About what?" I replied. Colleen related to me that when she was overwhelmed and stressed from work, she used this technique to get herself back on track. My life was so miserable at that point, I was willing to listen to just about any potentially helpful suggestion.

Within a day or two, I did an Internet search and found EFTUniverse.com, downloaded the mini-manual (see Chapter 4), lapped up the information, digested it, and tried the techniques—albeit initially skeptical and thinking to myself, "Nothing can work as well as this says it does. I'm a nurse. I know better."

But God had a bigger and better plan, something I never expected, a gift of miraculous healing from Him— finally.

My husband, Brad, was my first "client" and God gave us a "one-minute wonder." Brad was about to undergo vein stripping on his legs. He hates needles and this procedure is performed using a local anesthetic. I finally realized a day or so before the procedure how anxious he was, so I then inquired if he would like to try tapping (the informal term for EFT because you tap gently with your fingertips on specific points on the hands, face, and upper torso). It didn't take much to convince him.

I got out my instruction sheets and we began using Emotional Freedom Techniques (EFT) for the first time. Within minutes, his eyes turned into great big saucers, wide in amazement. I stopped tapping and asked what was going on with him. Stunned, Brad reported that his anxiety was gone. He also reported, "So is the chest pain"—chest pain I didn't even know he had.

EFT now had my full attention.

(Note: Brad has never had a recurrence of his anxiety or chest pain when faced with further leg procedures and he's probably had another dozen or more since that first EFT experience.)

Shortly thereafter, our friend Joan had throat surgery and stayed with us postoperatively. Joan had a terrible headache along with accompanying nausea the evening after her operation. Lying on the sofa, she asked me to tell her what I had learned about EFT. So I did.

After sharing the EFT synopsis, I asked if she wanted to try tapping. "Why not? It either works or I have to take another pain pill for this headache," Joan answered.

So Joan and I tapped. I don't have any recollection as to what her exact words were, but the second instance of a "one-minute wonder" occurred! Now God *really* had my attention! What in the world was going on here, I wondered. Joan's headache disappeared immediately, along with her nausea. Neither of those symptoms returned for the remainder of her 5-day stay with us. In fact, she felt so good the next morning, off we went to a rummage sale!

The following April, I took Dawson Church's Minneapolis EFT Universe classes (Levels 1 & 2), then completed the intermediate certification as an EFT practitioner (EFT-INT) and began working on the expert practitioner certification (EFT-EXP), tapping with anyone I could find, and all the while tapping furiously on my own negative stuff, never realizing how much there was that needed to be released.

I sought the help of Irene Baum, EFT-INT, in Milwaukee. I have no idea how I would have succeeded without her help in clearing out my painful past. Today, I'm a certified EFT practitioner and EFT Universe trainer.

Probably about a year after I earned my EFT-INT, I was driving to my friend Sarah's house to spend some time with her. During that short 10-minute drive, the Holy Spirit triggered a 20-year-old memory I had totally forgotten. I suspect I was tapping my thumbs on the steering wheel, praying, singing to Christian radio, and driving all at once—God talks to me at some odd times while I'm tapping!

The memory involved my beloved brother, Bill who was studying at Dickinson Law School in Pennsylvania shortly after Brad and I were married in 1991. I recalled a conversation Bill and I had at the time about his interest in becoming involved from a legal perspective with a pro-life magazine. He had been active before law school in the pro-life movement in Texas, even getting himself jailed once for chaining himself to an abortion clinic door. Bill and I discussed having me do the research he needed at Marquette Law Library. I told him to figure out a way to get me into the library and I would be happy to help him. Well, in the end, nothing came of the project, as law students tend not to have much extra time on their hands and Bill was also married with a family by then.

As a result of that discussion, however, I sent a note to our father in which I said something akin to "Dad, someday Bill and I will do something to change the world, something God needs us to do."

By the morning of that drive to Sarah's, God had already delivered the concept of Christian EFT to my mind. Recalling that thought all those years later, I suspect my mouth dropped open, and I started to cry. "Oh my, God, you took those words of mine literally," I said aloud in the car. I felt a great big lump in my chest and a thump in my heart as I realized that sentence written to my dad just might be the truth of this remembered revelation. Sadly, it was Bill's death that had been the impetus for me launching into EFT, so it turned out we did "do this together" after all!

I learned the lesson taught by those smarter than I that we really must watch the words that come out of our mouths—positive or negative—as the subconscious will make them our reality!

"An anxious heart weighs a man down, but a good word makes him glad" (Prov. 12:25).

EFT has wrought many miracles in my life. Longstanding obstacles, rooted in deep self-esteem issues, have vanished. Activities I would never have considered trying, I now do without thinking: playing volleyball, taking golf lessons, lifting weights alongside men at the local gym, eating with chopsticks, public speaking, teaching EFT, and writing a book! EFT has removed all of the self-conscious barriers blocking my way, imparting to me a full life. Now at age 62, I feel like a kid again!

"And we know that in all things God works for the good of those who love him, who have been called according to his purpose" (Rom. 8:28).

Today, I stand here with a tiny bit of sadness remaining, knowing I'm so very alive and the painful loss of my siblings, Bill and Karen, spawned this emotional healing for me. In tears, the realization dawned on me that I cared for them all their lives: Karen for her too-short 17 months of life as she battled biliary atresia, and Bill, especially at the end when he needed someone to be there for his every need. I have no regret for the time I gave each of them; it was my pleasure to do so on their behalf. The sad pain comes in knowing that, with their deaths, they repaid the favor and cared for me in return. It was through losing the two of them and the resulting burden of grief that I experienced a much-needed emotional healing and a rebirth of sorts, by the grace of God, through EFT.

Good-bye, my pretties — I loved you with all my heart and still do, and I miss you both every day. I hope to make you proud and allow you to see that your early deaths were not in vain. It all served a much higher purpose than any of us could have imagined. I stand amazed, and look forward to being reunited with you in heaven where we will celebrate together! God be praised. Amen.

Rest in Peace

Karen Marie Rice

25 June 1960–29 November 1961

William Gregg Rice, Esq.

26 September 1961–28 August 2010

*Then said he, "I am going to my Father's; and though with
great difficulty I am got hither, yet now I do not repent me of all
the trouble I have been at to arrive where I am. My sword I give
to him that shall succeed me in my pilgrimage, and my courage
and skill to him that can get it. My marks and scars I carry
with me, to be a witness for me that I have fought His battles
who now will be my rewarder...." So he passed over, and
all the trumpets sounded for him on the other side.*

—John Bunyan, *Pilgrim's Progress,*
Part 2: Christiana

Ultimately, I've learned the lesson well that God
wastes nothing. All my life experiences have led to this
moment. I didn't like much of it, but my heavenly Father
surely knew best, as always. My new life has begun,
having embarked on continuing to serve Him as He so
deems through sharing and teaching the healing mechanism EFT.

Emotionally, God delivered this remarkable gift to me
when I needed it most. He spared my life, using EFT. It
has opened a whole new world for me. It has given me a
tool for clearing out past negative emotions and the physical manifestations of them. And this path to a new life of
abundance and profound healing can be yours too!

Interested? Please read on.

Keep in mind, however, that EFT is *not* a substitute
for medical help from a qualified physician. Please take
responsibility for your own health and well-being.

2

EFT and God's Created Physiology

Christians sometimes become a bit dismayed when various energy practitioners begin explaining how these techniques work, including EFT, via reference to Chinese medicine. Chinese medicine actually does have a basis in anatomy and physiology, which Western science has now proven through research. Although EFT can be explained via the energy pathways of the body, or "meridians," as they are called in Chinese medicine, I hope to give you a good flavor of the physiological way God created us. I hope you find it as interesting as I have!

The Body's Chemicals

For an emotion to be felt, the body must mix up a specific neurochemical compound from all the "ligands" available from which it can choose. A ligand (a word created by the late Dr. Candace Pert) can be a neurotransmitter, a peptide, or a hormone. Some of the neurotransmitters are norepinephrine, dopamine, serotonin, histamine, adenosine and ATP (adenosine triphosphate), glutamate, aspartate, GABA, glycine, acetylcholine, anandamide, and nitric oxide. Peptides are insulin, amino acids, and proteins, and these comprise over 90% of the ligand group. The third group of ligands consists of the reproductive hormones. It's surely an interesting mix of chemicals that goes into producing a single emotion!

The first time you experience any emotion, for example, sadness, your body mixes up a special potion of these aforementioned chemicals. Your body then memorizes the recipe so the next time an event happens to you that is similar to the one that triggered the emotion (e.g., sadness), your body will once again concoct that same neurochemical mix, giving you that exact same feeling (the sadness). The body uses this mechanism for each different emotion or feeling you experience, but it takes this one step further. You also tend to feel the emotion somatically, that is, somewhere in your body. It could be in the stomach, thus the "butterflies" you feel when fear or anxiety sets in, or perhaps it is a tightening in your chest when a feeling of resentment or anger comes calling.

Every time you experience a new emotional event, your subconscious scours your experiential database hoping to find some similar incident to compare the new one to, and when it does, your body stirs up that special emotional chemical mixture again. Each time this happens, the emotion gets reinforced, making those habitual neural bundles where the "recipe" is stored thicker and heavier. Sadness compounds sadness, fear compounds fear, trapping you, reinforcing the trauma.

Your negative life memories aren't stored only in your mind, but also somewhere in your body—be it organs, muscles, tissues, bones, joints—thus the term "body mind." Science demonstrates that your subconscious, which put all those memories into those specific body parts, holds them well for you there, usually for about 10 to 40 years, and then it gives up the ghost because it cannot do the job anymore. The subconscious simply gets tired, and disease appears in whatever body part(s) is holding the destructive memory.

This mechanism can be likened to a computer. It's not the best analogy, but you'll get the idea. Your mind is like the CPU of your computer. Just as your CPU disperses fragments of documents you type all over the hard drive, your brain scatters pieces of memories all over your body, which is like the hard drive. Your subconscious runs 95% of your thinking processes (Lipton, 2008, p. 33), unbeknownst to your conscious mind. You have no idea what it is storing, what it thinks, how it feels, or pretty much anything at all about what is playing in your mind's background, ultimately running your life!

Our thinking and feeling consciousness is actually under the control of these early prerecorded habits derived from the perceptions acquired in our childhood experiences. In fact, the subconscious mind can be completely at odds with what our conscious mind thinks we want. An example would be making a commitment on New Year's Day to go to the gym three times a week. By the end of January, the trips to the gym have ended. Why? Because the subconscious mind overrode what the conscious mind knew to be a good thing to do. The subconscious mind nearly always wins. It overrides our conscious thinking processes and can be the seat of all of our self-sabotage. Like your computer's CPU, your subconscious runs everything from the background of your "body mind" with little or no input from your frontal cortex (the decision-making part of your brain).

How Fears and Feelings Affect Us

Today, other than in some rare, odd incident, most of the dangers we Westerners "encounter" are those we perceive in our own minds versus actual physical dangers. Typical contemporary fears might include getting fired tomorrow, anxiety that we may be underdressed for tonight's formal affair, anger because someone just cut us off in traffic, resentment because we feel Mom favors another sibling over us, or hate because of continual verbal abuse.

While your conscious mind is positive and excited about upcoming opportunities in life, your subconscious mind's recorded message—a message you may not even realize is playing—may be repeating, "You don't deserve it!" "You'll look foolish tonight," "That jerk could have killed me," "I hate so and so." Those messages are subverting your conscious mind and running your life via this subliminal background soundtrack.

Enter Clinical EFT, the best of the 250 energy modalities out there, in my personal and professional opinion (based on decades of nursing experience). Some of these other modalities, such as Reiki, chiropractic, or massage therapy, will alert you to the fact you have stored some negative memory in a body part, but practitioners of those techniques, unless specially trained in Clinical EFT, have little ability to help you consciously process or release that specific memory, extricating it from its hiding place in the subconscious realm. They can refer you to someone who might help, but processing the memory is not part of those particular practices.

Science explains how negative feelings get assigned to the different body parts. As the ligands enter the cellular receptors, a "feeling" is produced. Each ligand and cell receptor is like a key and lock. Only specific ligands can enter certain receptors. Dopamine cannot enter a serotonin receptor; only serotonin can. When the ligand finds the correct receptor and enters it, something akin to a dance is initiated as the cellular receptor is "unlocked."

As the vibration from EFT tapping occurs, it interchanges with those same cellular receptors, neutralizing the negative emotion trapped within them. EFT bypasses the conscious mind and disconnects the emotion or feeling from an experienced negative event. The even more exciting part is that the negative emotion tends to be permanently severed via this process. If all the "aspects" (details) around an event are found and properly neutralized, it's a done deal! I tell clients they will then relate the negative story as emotionlessly as reading a Dr. Seuss book to their children, as the memory will no longer have any hold over them. This results in light overcoming the darkness of the memory being addressed and it can then no longer stand. It has been exposed and healed, and is now a non-event!

Other physiological processes are involved in memory storage. The ligands don't just interact with a cell receptor, they also communicate with each other. Scientists once believed that each anatomical part had its own specific cell receptors. Research now shows that brain cell receptors are found in the gut and the bone marrow. So if you have a negative memory stored in your liver, that problem will also involve your endocrine, immune, and nervous systems, which are all intertwined, causing them problems too. In other words, because of the nature of ligands, all your body parts are in constant communication with each other. So if one organ is in distress, chances are others will soon be too.

Paul writes in 1 Corinthians 12:12, "The body is a unit, though it is made up of many parts; and though all its parts are many, they form one body. So it is with Christ. As it is, there are many parts, but one body."

Just as Jesus told us the Church is one body and every part is necessary for the function of the other parts, God the Father made our body in exactly this way too.

As the majority of the neuropeptide cellular receptors are found in the limbic system, Dr. Candace Pert referred to them as "molecules of emotion" (Pert, 1997, p. 21). The limbic system is our emotional center, located in the brain, and its primary components are the amygdala, hippocampus, and hypothalamus (other components are the thalamus, cingulate gyrus, and basal ganglia). The limbic system is where most of our sensory input collides with the nervous system. The immune system is also directly connected to the neuropeptide receptors, showing without a doubt that our immune system takes a direct hit from all things emotional.

According to Dr. Caroline Leaf (2008, p. 3), "At any one moment, your brain is creatively performing about 400 billion actions, of which you are only conscious of around 2,000." Our conscious mind only processes a tiny portion of what we see, think, smell, touch, or do, filing away the remainder wherever it decides to file it, making it inaccessible to us and to our thinking mind—that's a lot of bits of extraneous information for the subconscious to wreak havoc with!

Dr. Leaf elaborated that 87% of illnesses are connected to our thoughts and emotions. Other factors, such as our diet, genetics, and environment, account for the remaining 13% (Leaf, 2008, p. 5). This surely demonstrates that the body and mind are completely integrated. We are literally what we think. Proverbs 23:7 backs up this truth: "For as he thinks in his heart, so is he."

The subconscious mind also puts into deep storage a host of negative memories, particularly the repetitive ones. If it didn't, you would be completely overwhelmed emotionally and mentally, and probably unable to function at all. It's these "buried" negative emotions that cause many of our problems, running our life decisions without us knowing the subconscious is doing so. If your negative emotional base is set back in some awful memory from when you were 4 years old, say, then your subconscious is still probably running your life the way that 4-year-old did. Incredible, isn't it?

How EFT Works on Our Memories

We can use EFT to root out those early childhood memories, delivering them into the conscious realm where we can deal with them rationally, freeing us to live life in a more calm, relaxed, and adult manner — or as EFT researcher Dawson Church, PhD, says, "As adults today, we parent ourselves."

Your subconscious is like a computer or DVR playing a recorded movie. You can passively view the same scenes again and again until you decide to change the movie. In the same way, your subconscious will play that same negative emotional movie clip over and over until EFT erases the file and replaces it in your subconscious with a new and positive one.

Please note that the truth here is not actually a factor. Instead, this simply has to do with how you *feel*. It's all about individual perception. With negative perception of an event, a memory can be caught in a negative cognitive feedback loop. This is why your emotional health can seem like someone else's fault, but it really isn't. Your emotional health is your own interpretation of what the world looks like to you. Astonishingly, it may have no reality basis whatsoever! Don't take this the wrong way please — you aren't "crazy" if your interpretation has been plaguing you, just human!

As much as we might prefer to, it actually isn't fair to blame our parents, grandparents, relatives, teachers, or friends for how we feel today (although most of us engage in this blame game from time to time).

EFT is the portal to the subconscious to diffuse and record over those very old movies playing in our minds! Once I have disabled the emotions around certain issues, those issues are no longer relevant. I've been disconnected from the emotions previously associated with them. The emotions no longer have a hold on me, and I will most likely never be bothered again by the matter, provided I do my EFT tapping thoroughly, dismantling all the pieces (aspects, in EFT parlance) of that issue. The science behind Emotional Freedom Techniques teaches us how those early childhood experiences hold us fast, creating our adult reality without us ever understanding what makes us tick. The subconscious grabs an idea and stays with it throughout our lives until we realize life isn't giving us what we want, expect, or think we deserve. For those of us who use EFT, we know we can dismantle those early cognitive beliefs, changing limiting and/or perplexing thoughts. We are then equipped to move forward, newly empowered by a healthy, positive outlook.

Now let's move on to the primary substance underlying stress: cortisol.

The Role of Cortisol

Why does excitement in our lives make us feel alive? What causes the buzz we feel when we are participating in stressful things, or when something is upsetting us?

The answer to both questions is stress hormones. Adrenaline (also called epinephrine), cortisol, and norepinephrine (also called noradrenaline) are the three major stress hormones triggered by our limbic brain when excitement or trouble happens. Cortisol keeps our brain in a beta activity state, that is, a heightened awareness of thinking and feeling. It keeps us active and moving.

One morning in the midst of days of intensive work on this book, both my computer and another one receiving edits, stopped doing their job. Suddenly missing from my computer was a key folder that contained all 22 years of gathered data on family genealogy, family pictures, historical files, mission material, EFT training material, and text/case studies for this book. Everything was completely gone! Both computers had been functioning fine the evening before. Suddenly, neither computer was usable for the *EFT for Christians* book editing, let alone anything else.

This was stress in a big way. I can guarantee my cortisol level was seriously elevated. I was in a high beta stress level, trying to think my way out of this problem — how was I going to replace the book? Could I find all the lost pieces, retrieving them from e-mails? What would happen if I couldn't find the pieces? As even the original unedited manuscript was gone, was I going to have to start all over again? I began to pray, "Okay, God, this is your book — You need to find that file," and I began to tap. I called my friend Carol to back me up in prayer because it was her computer on the receiving end that wasn't working either. She prayed phrases such as, "Lifting the impossible up to the possible" (where God does His best work), "Let nothing hinder the purpose You have with this book," "All right, God, it's in Your hands," and tapping on emotions such as "fear" and "uncertainty."

I knew the enemy was at work. I had already lost the entire month of April to an upper respiratory infection, necessitating a couple doctor visits and a course of antibiotics. The week before the computer fiasco, another "cold" had appeared on my scene, and I rarely get sick! And now this?

Here was a perfect use of EFT in a high-stress situation, sealing it all with a blanket of prayer, lowering my cortisol and adrenaline levels, sending the blood flowing back into my prefrontal cortex, so that I could think once more. In spite of the initial immense fear I had experienced, I actually stayed pretty calm. I knew God was my only rescue here, and tapping was His way of settling down my physical body after the initial shock of realizing all my hard work was gone! Praise God, He thinks of everything! Cortisol and the other stress chemicals all play into the limbic system, and my levels had gone off the chart in response to this computer incident. (Mercifully, the files could be retrieved from an offsite storage backup service.)

The limbic system was created by God to keep us safe from predators and other bodily threats. If a loud, unexplained noise occurs, the amygdala, an almond-shaped mass of nuclei located deep within the brain, sends an alarm throughout the body via an intricate system of nerve and hormonal signals, prompting the adrenal glands to release a flood of hormones, including adrenaline and cortisol. The fight, flight, or freeze (FFF) mechanism has just been activated, keeping us alert and aroused, watching for danger.

Our heart rate increases, blood pressure is elevated, glucose is released to the tissues, blood leaves the neocortex of the brain for the larger muscles in the legs in case flight is necessary, digestion is interrupted (no time to eat now!), the immune system literally slows down, sex and growth are out of the question at the moment as survival is the utmost goal in the body's mind. Estrogen, testosterone, and the neurotransmitters dopamine and serotonin are also involved to a lesser extent in this sometimes life-and-death struggle. All nonessential bodily functions slow down until the dangerous situation resolves itself.

This survival mechanism was implanted only for short-term use. The limbic FFF is activated, the immediate problem gets resolved, and the stress hormones return to normal levels, dropping the heart rate and glucose levels back to normal. DHEA (dehydroepiandrosterone, a healing chemical) levels are restored from their depressed levels to increase body repair and growth, allowing the immune system to take over, maintaining good health. The stress hormones and DHEA cannot be maintained at high levels at the same time. Either DHEA is at an adequate level and stress hormones are down, or stress hormones are elevated and DHEA is low. We simply cannot heal when we are stressed!

Obviously, the best scenario for our bodies is to have low stress hormones, eliminating all the wear and tear on us. God didn't create the human body to live in high stress for long periods of time, but we now have EFT to aid in addressing these patterns of chronic stress and keeping ourselves healthy. EFT will bring stress hormone levels down, as do other relaxation techniques. Research found that cortisol blood levels dropped 24% after an hour session of EFT tapping (Church, Yount, & Brooks, 2012).

Without intervention, it may take days for stress hormone levels to return to normal, especially when the body is under chronic stress. Nowadays, we humans often remain in this high state of alert because of the high-functioning lifestyles we lead, and many times this is by choice. We actually become addicted to elevated stress levels, leaving us feeling sad and uncomfortable when we begin to slow down for a short period of time. Once accustomed to high stress levels, the subconscious tends to want to keep us there. It has become our standard modus operandi. In fact, the subconscious will even put us in situations to provoke an increased stress level, keeping the hormones and glucose at higher levels—we truly become addicted to those chemicals!

We may think we feel relaxed, but often we continue in that high beta brain wave state. It's typical of modern life. Unfortunately, it is killing us—*literally, killing us*. Our bodies simply weren't designed for long-term FFF activation. Continuous high levels of cortisol are known to cause major physical problems, including increased abdominal fat, weight gain, obesity, memory impairment, heart disease, adrenal fatigue, and diabetes.

Since most of us no longer face genuine physically threatening situations, the threats are really just "paper tigers"—they're simply all in your mind. Due to the physiology of the brain, particularly the limbic system, your mind can't distinguish between a real physical threat and the one you create in your own imagination. Imagination itself can trigger FFF with all its heart-thumping, perspiring, and agitated, frightened reaction. When you awaken from a nightmare in a puddle of sweat accompanied by palpitations, you have just activated the FFF in that dream.

A case in point: the body treats worry just the same as it treats a genuinely dangerous threat. So worrying about the boss firing you versus the boss actually firing you triggers the exact same chemical release in your body. Each situation appears to be the same to your mind during your thinking and feeling process and either can set off the FFF mechanism. The limbic system doesn't differentiate between perceived and real situations. Worry is stress, as we all know. Over time, that same worry will break down your body, causing physical illnesses.

Your mind tells your body what to believe. Real threats or perceived threats are reacted to in exactly the same manner. Your personality and thoughts comprise your present reality—all the learned emotions of the past constitute your feelings and habits in the present. Ninety percent of your thoughts today were thoughts of yesterday, and they all lead to the same behavior today. All of your feelings and emotions are end products of previous experiences. Emotions drive events in your life, making your thoughts a reality. For the most part, your body is your unconscious mind living in the past, creating tomorrow to be exactly the same future as yesterday. We literally become what we think.

There are instances of patients in hospitals who willed themselves to die within hours of a fatal diagnosis given to them by a doctor, and they did. If you desire something enough, your subconscious will grant you that desire. EFT can be used to discard our limiting thoughts, and our feelings around them, so God can create a healthier reality for us. We use His EFT process, and then sit back and watch Him work it out for us — EFT helps us get out of His way!

EFT's Use by Professional Athletes

Psychologist Dr. Erin Shannon (herself the daughter of a pro athlete) has seen significant success in treating professional athletes from the National Football League (NFL), National Hockey League (NHL), and Major League Baseball (MLB) with EFT. Dr. Shannon also extols the benefits she regularly sees in her practice when utilizing EFT with her patients and draws the distinction between these "rapid results and deep healing vs. just understanding and coping with their problems," as with "talk therapy" (Edes, 2011). Other documented incidents of professional athletes utilizing EFT can be readily sourced online and in *EFT for Sports Performance*, by Jessica A. Howard.

APA Standards for Empirically Validated Treatments

EFT Universe supports the evidence-based standards defined by the American Psychological Association (APA) Division 12 (Clinical Psychology) Task Force ("APA standards," for short). These define an "empirically validated treatment" as one for which there are two different controlled trials conducted by independent research teams.

For a treatment to be designated "efficacious," the studies must demonstrate that the treatment is better than a wait list, placebo, or established efficacious treatment.

To be designated "probably efficacious," a treatment must have been shown to be better than a wait list in two studies that meet these criteria, or are conducted by the same research team rather than two independent teams.

The APA standards advocate that studies contain sufficient subjects to achieve a level of statistical significance of $p < .05$ or greater, which means that there is only 1 possibility in 20 that the results are due to chance.

The current status of EFT as an "evidence-based" practice is summarized in this statement published in the APA journal *Review of General Psychology*:

A literature search identified 51 peer-reviewed papers that report or investigate clinical outcomes following the tapping of acupuncture points to address psychological issues. The 18 randomized controlled trials in this sample were critically evaluated for design quality, leading to the conclusion that they consistently demonstrated strong effect sizes and other positive statistical results that far exceed chance after relatively few treatment sessions. Criteria for evidence-based treatments proposed by Division 12 of the American Psychological Association were also applied and found to be met for a number of conditions, including PTSD. (Feinstein, 2012, pp. 364–380)

Summary

With all the new science, the once mystical is now demystified. EFT interrupts negative thought processes, and then uses these scientific processes to clear and reprogram the neural pathways to shift us into a positive direction of thinking and acting that will restore and maintain our health. As we tap, shifts begin to happen in the brain. EFT recalibrates the brain, slowing it down, so the prefrontal cortex can think, bringing coherence into life. We think before we act. We live mindfully, changing our internal state of being. Our minds are quiet. There is no longer the need to consume huge quantities of alcohol, food, or drugs to get us through the day. EFT quiets us so we no longer feel the need to use these other things to try and calm us down or drown out our negative thoughts.

Tapping changes how we feel. God changes our perception and perspectives. Christian EFT is like an expanded prayer. These techniques allow us to feel and actually hear God talking to us. Our creativity comes alive once again. Now when our emotions manifest our reality, it is a calmer, less selfish reality. We become conscious of our thoughts, which shines light into our once dark, gloomy lives where we were simply going through the motions of living. We are truly alive again!

This is the intersection of science and emotion. When we quiet ourselves, turning inward to view who we really are, feel what we were meant to feel, we turn off those disease genes. Our conscious thoughts pull the emotion out of events, pouring light into that darkness. We release the gunk clogging up cellular receptors all through our bodies. Our physical self begins to heal as our organs once again function optimally. This is faith and science working sublimely together. Science and faith are not at odds. Instead, they complement each other.

This harmonious state is how God created our bodies to thrive. We were never meant to live in a perpetually high state of stress, a state brought about at times by our own sinfulness. In these instances, as we confess and begin clearing our physical bodies using EFT, we find ourselves in a much healthier and happier place.

EFT is a gift from God, and I've witnessed its amazing track record of success firsthand. Having used it routinely in my own life, I can personally testify that it has brought me a joy and peace I never thought possible. It's the joy and peace I prayed God would give me for nearly four decades. Finally, He answered my prayer by introducing me to EFT.

> *...for I am the Lord, who heals you.*
> (Exod. 15:26)

I'd like to pay that forward by introducing you to the same process: Emotional Freedom Techniques, or what is now called Clinical EFT.

3

10 Common Misconceptions
Christians Have about EFT

Christian EFT is a new idea based on Clinical EFT, and as with anything new, many fears and doubts arise, but these are often based on ignorance, resistance, or personal biases. "Christ, in whom are hidden all the treasures of wisdom and knowledge" (Col. 2:3).

With Christian EFT now being adopted into the energy modality sphere, questions arise from Believers who are curious or uncertain about the use of this technique, its effectiveness, and whether this practice is acceptable for use by Christians.

Having been redeemed by Jesus at age 22, been a registered nurse for 41 years, and a certified advanced EFT practitioner for a number of years now, it's my heartfelt conviction that God will utilize this simple but powerful breakthrough technique to deliver a new era of healing to His people going forward. I have heard many people express their concern, doubt, and skepticism about what EFT can accomplish long-term.

As this book is written specifically for fellow Believers, let me take a bit of time here and address the main misconceptions I have encountered among Christians in my practice and elsewhere regarding EFT and how it fits into our walk with Jesus. EFT is indeed a "new" gift that needs to be explained so as to be understood—and my earnest prayer is that it will be brought to our churches, who can then engage practitioners to work with God's people to bring the healing benefits of EFT to those who are hurting, both physically and emotionally.

Misconception #1:
EFT is one of those New Age things.

New Age beliefs espouse being "like God," part of His creative force, a creature wanting to liken him or herself to the all-creating God, or to participate in the process as one who is equal to God. This is what Adam and Eve did in the Garden of Eden when they believed Satan's temptation. ("Your eyes will be opened and you will be like God knowing good and evil," Gen. 3:5; "The eyes of both were opened," Gen. 3:7). In contrast, Christian EFT instead acknowledges God as the Creator and God of the universe, sole Healer, and Provider. God is personal and He is in communication with the people of His making. He wants to see us whole and healed. He is Jehovah Rophe, God of Healing. We seek to walk in His Will ("The Lord's will be done," Acts 21:14); God heals ("Jesus Christ heals you," Acts 9:34); we are healed solely through Him as His disciples, not through our own power, as New Age adherents believe.

Misconception #2: EFT is a satanic practice.

This is an easy misconception to dispel. Satan destroys. God heals. Satan, in any way he can within our bodies, souls, and spirits, wants to stop God's activities and His Will from being done. Utilizing Christian EFT, we're more fully equipped to receive healing in body, soul, and spirit so we can continue in the Will of God and strive toward our mission of bringing His kingdom on earth as it is in heaven (the Lord's Prayer). There is not one example in Holy Scripture of Satan healing anyone; he is not in the healing business. Only God is. And of course, scripture shows us multiple examples of Jesus' healing power. "He sent them out to proclaim the kingdom of God and to heal the sick" (Luke 9:2). Miraculous healings were a central part of his ministry during His time here on earth.

EFT is part of the new mind-body paradigm. Science developed over the past two to three decades clearly shows there is a direct connection, as Scripture teaches, between the body, soul, mind, heart, and spirit. The Bible teaches this in the "Great Commandment" (Matt. 22:37–40) "Jesus replied: 'Love the Lord your God with all your heart and with all our soul and with all your mind.' This is the first and greatest commandment. And the second is like it: 'Love your neighbor as yourself.' All the law and the prophets hang on these two commandments."

EFT lends itself to this commandment. As we use EFT to clear our emotional baggage, we are then better equipped to embrace the subsequent commandments Jesus taught us.

For example, forgiveness is a hallmark of EFT. As the negative emotions are neutralized via tapping, forgiveness for both ourselves and those who harmed us settles in. Many times following an EFT session, love streams right in on forgiveness's coattails. To me, it is a perfect modality for use within the Christian church, fulfilling Jesus' commandment to us, "Be kind and compassionate to one another, forgiving each other, just as in Christ God forgave you" (Eph. 4:32).

Misconception #3:
EFT is connected to Chinese religion.

Chinese medicine and Chinese religion are two entirely different things. Eastern religion is *not* part of EFT. Religious discussions are not part of any EFT class curriculum. If "religion" is discussed in a class, it is an opinion of a student or the instructor. When I originally came to EFT, that was one of my primary concerns too, so I was on alert for anything "religious" in the classes I took. In hundreds of hours of EFT instruction, I've never seen anything in the official curriculum that contradicts our Christian faith.

Chinese medicine has been in existence for over 5,000 years. It utilizes the meridian system to explain energy flow. (There are 12 primary meridians, or energy channels, in the body.) Our complexly made bodies do indeed contain energy/electricity, as you have experienced firsthand after shuffling across a carpet and then receiving an electrical shock when you touch something or someone. Illness is a result of disturbances in that energy flow. Needles utilized in acupuncture return the flow to normal.

In Christian EFT, there are no needles. In EFT, we are able to tap and release any "energy" blockages, thus reinvigorating God's creativeness that was so lovingly placed into our bodies by our Creator himself. We are made in His image with all of the wonders and beauty that entails ("So God made man in His own image," Gen. 1:27). Our various body systems are only one part of a very intricate and marvelous work, constructed by a wise and creative God.

Christian EFT uses God's Word as a foundation. God is very active through it and through our bodies as vessels of His Spirit. EFT can go into every part of the body, our emotions, and our subconscious minds, neutralizing feelings and memories that are stuck within us. The tapping exercises can bring a change and resolution to short-term as well as long-term problems.

The Chinese medicine reference is only one way to explain how EFT works. As a Christian, I prefer to explain how God heals us through His creation of our anatomy and physiology. Today, with much newly discovered science, Christians can completely ignore the Eastern medicine explanation of EFT if they choose to do so ("He sent them out...to heal the sick," Luke 9:2; "Just say the word and your servant will be healed," Matt. 8:8).

Misconception #4: EFT is part of the Hindu faith because it uses something like the chakras.

Christian EFT bears the unwavering message that Jesus is the Way, the Truth, and the Life (John 14:1). We talk to God, pray to Him, sing to Him, meditate on Him, use Bible affirmations to communicate and reestablish our bond with Him that was secured by the atoning work of Jesus on the Cross. The Holy Spirit is the prime communicator between God and humans during tapping. Through EFT, we are opened to the Holy Spirit who can work His miracles and blessings upon our lives ("One who came from the Father full of grace and truth," John 1:14; "You will know the Truth and the truth will make you free," John 8:32). While EFT zeroes in on physical acupressure points to provide healing, this should not be confused with the more mystical belief in chakras, which are instead considered centers of spiritual power in the human body.

Misconception #5: EFT is about healing yourself, which goes against God.

Healing ourselves is not considered scriptural. Self-healing is a form of self-promotion. It is a sin and an offense against God, who reconciles us through the work of Jesus. We Christians cannot take credit for healing because only God heals. Healing is under His purview, not ours. Christian EFT relies on God Himself as our healer because God created us. Our bodies can be healed because He instilled this healing mechanism in us. It is not of our own doing. We bear witness to the truth that

He is the One who cleanses, heals, and provides the way to a renewed life. We are a new creature ("If anyone is in Christ, he is a new creature," 2 Cor. 5:17). Ego is out of the way. We can have a renewed purpose and one filled with abundance and joy in Him through EFT ("Restore to me the joy of Your salvation," Ps. 51:12; "Made new in the attitude of your mind," Eph. 4:23).

Misconception #6: EFT goes against the Bible.

Christian EFT uses the apostolic direction that Jesus issued to all of His disciples who choose to learn and to follow Him ("Your kingdom come, Your will be done on earth as it is in heaven," Luke 11:2). When negative issues are removed, and the bite of a disturbing incident and its charge is neutralized, we can then move forward to fulfill and follow God's Will as directed by Jesus Himself, pointing us toward a new purpose in our life's walk with Him. The past is truly past and we can look ahead in awaiting God's personalized direction for our future. He calls us to an abundant life ("I came that they might have life and have it to the full," John 10:10). Other scriptural versions use the word "abundantly" here instead of the word "full." I don't believe this blessing to be solely a reference to an abundant spiritual life, but to an abundantly healthy physical life as well.

Illnesses and emotional pain don't lead any of us to feel abundantly blessed. My own personal testimony of EFT is that I'm living, breathing proof it can deliver emotional abundance, joy, peace, and happiness in Christ. God has given us an amazing process in EFT. And if you'll utilize these simple-to-do techniques, I believe a powerful blessing from God awaits you ("My God will meet all your needs," Phil. 4:19; "Seek first His kingdom…all these things will be given to you," Matt. 6:33).

Misconception #7: EFT is connected to the occult.

The dictionary.com definition of the occult is: "of or pertaining to magic, astrology, or any system claiming use or knowledge of secret or supernatural powers or agencies; beyond the range of ordinary knowledge or understanding; mysterious; secret; disclosed or communicated only to the initiated; hidden from view."

The practice of EFT fits nothing in this definition whatsoever. There is no secret knowledge. It is pure science based upon God's design of our anatomy. Anyone and everyone can learn how to tap. There is nothing hidden from view. There is no religious content taught, unless so disclosed, in EFT classes. Even in Christian EFT, the tapping format is the same format used by all those utilizing Clinical EFT. What changes in Christian EFT is the wording. We elect to incorporate our own belief system while we tap ("We preach Christ crucified," I Cor. 1:23).

Embracing the same foundation of Clinical EFT, any other religious group could do the same thing, which is why I'm advocating that other faith-based EFT adherents write their own books, incorporating their religious teachings into their tapping protocols, such as *EFT for Jews* and *EFT for Muslims*.

Misconception #8: EFT goes against the Christian way that we're supposed to suffer.

Some Christian sects think we have to suffer in order to be accepted by God, or that suffering is natural because Jesus and the apostles suffered. But we Christians know that any suffering we try to embrace will still never be good enough, and 2 Corinthians 12:9 teaches us, "My grace is sufficient." There is no pain or suffering we can offer to God that will atone for anything we have done wrong. Isaiah (64:6) teaches us, "All our righteous acts are as filthy rags." We cannot add to what Jesus has already done on the Cross. And He specifically said on the Cross, "It is finished" (John 19:30). Our salvation is therefore complete. There is nothing more to do. The Law has been wholly fulfilled by the sacrifice provided by the Blood of the Lamb.

Christian EFT acknowledges that we are made whole because Jesus made us whole. This wholeness is for our body, soul, and spirit. We are to accept that free gift from God, and pass it on to others by teaching them to use EFT. EFT helps wash away and eliminate ill effects from our body, soul, and spirit, so we can be renewed, refreshed, and reinvigorated to move outside ourselves and more fully into the world to help others. Jesus was our perfect example in His ministry ("Wash me and I will be as white as snow," Ps. 51:7; "He died to sin once for all," Rom. 6:10).

Misconception #9: EFT may be sinful or harmful.

Christian EFT is based on a loving, personal, transcendent God who calls people to repentance and acceptance of Jesus as their personal Savior. He is established as the Energy-Giver and the Almighty Source of all healing. Christ-centered EFT always gives God the glory ("By grace you have been saved," Eph. 2:5; "Salvation is found in no one else, for there is no other name under heaven given to mankind by which we must be saved," Acts 4:12).

Misconception #10:
Tapping looks just too odd to be real.

Tapping does look odd initially to some people. However, it is simply needle-less acupuncture, although it actually imparts a significantly broader scope of healing, which is why it is sometimes called "emotional acupuncture." The tapping concentrates our focus on the different areas we need to hone in on, the concerns and feelings, the words we are saying, the places in our bodies that are central to the pain(s) we are feeling — both emotional and physical. Tapping gets our attention, physically as well as emotionally.

Tapping can have a humbling effect on us because it works so well and the act of allowing it to work on us is humbling. Many have worked for years to clear these negative emotions only to find that a few hours of tapping is more effective. Frankly, EFT just seems to be too simple to work as well as it does. However, that's the ultimate beauty of it—its simplicity! God's love and His offer of salvation are so simple too. Both EFT and Salvation are free. All we need to do is receive them as the blessed gifts from God they each are.

Summary

Christian EFT is sympathetic, compassionate, and presents the truth with gentleness and respect ("Always be prepared to give an answer…but do it with gentleness and respect," 1 Pet. 3:15), just as Jesus did. What better faith to embrace and teach this healing and restorative practice than Christians?

Some Christians believe miraculous healing ended when the apostolic age was over. This is patently false. Missionaries around the world constantly report incidents of God healing His people and even raising them from the dead. We Christians in the United States seem to be a more difficult sell on these remarkable modern-day examples of heavenly healing. We just don't see it happening here as it does in Third World countries; however God's healing is alive and actively working until the end of time when all illnesses of body, soul, or spirit will be eliminated once and for all. EFT is a tool of healing now in use by God—just as He has delivered healing via the practice of medicine and surgery through the ages—and I won't be surprised if EFT healing ministries begin to pop up in congregations all over the world, including America, once its benefits are fully understood and quantified as useful in blessing and healing Christians who are hurting.

Christian EFT utilizes Scripture. It is based on the eternal Word and Truth of God. The power of EFT is magnified significantly by incorporating these scriptural affirmations while tapping. The ideas, practice, substance, and background of Christian EFT all lead back to a basic Christian principle: namely, knowing God and following His Word. All material, affirmations to tap with, everything is based upon teachings from the Bible, its content, its power, its truth, its gift to us from the Father and Giver of all good things.

I do not make this statement lightly. EFT needs to be given a chance as it is such a powerful tool for negating the emotions that clog and block God's natural healing of our bodies. The walls of sin can so easily put up barriers to that healing. There may be times when we need to seek help from the medical professionals God has blessed us with, like the early physician, Saint Luke. We should pray, seeking God's guidance as to what kind of healing help we need. Allow God to guide you to the correct resource. Seek medical help when that help is appropriate.

Surely we cannot box God in or say healing only took place "back in Bible times." He is as active and moving today as He has always been ("Jesus Christ is the same yesterday, today, and forever," Heb. 13:8).

I am hoping the contents of this book will make Christian EFT a commonly used resource in churches, a source of cleansing and healing, giving us another reason to express thankfulness and praise to God for this easy technique that can be learned and applied to so many areas of our life.

4

The EFT Mini-Manual

The following is a reprint of *The EFT Mini-Manual* by Dawson Church, which you can also download for free at EFTUniverse.com. The manual will tell you everything you need to know to get started with EFT now.

Stress and the Power of Emotional Healing

You've taken the leap, and decided to find out more about EFT! You're not alone. Over a million people have selected *The EFT Manual* as a primary healing resource, and EFT is found in many countries around the globe. EFT is in hospitals, psychotherapy clinics, sports fields, business coaching practices, families, and many other places. What is EFT and why is it so popular?

EFT is a very quick and simple method of reducing the intensity of traumatic memories. Everyone who lives on planet Earth had at least some trauma growing up. For the lucky ones, these traumatic events were rare and mild, like a nurse forgetting, for a few minutes, to give you a bottle when you were a baby. For some people, the traumatic events of their childhoods were horrific, like genocide, rape, or war. Most of us fall somewhere between these two extremes. Over the years we've built up a backlog of traumatic memories, reinforced by negative experiences as young adults. By the time we're in full adulthood, we've formed behaviors and coping strategies based on these experiences. Our emotional growth has been shaped by them, and we may believe we're destined to remain that way for the rest of our lives.

Historically, it was very difficult to shape our emotional experience. A person could spend years in contemplation or meditation, cultivating inner peace. But that state is easily disturbed by the events of the average day. These techniques take many years to learn and perfect.

EFT has ushered in a whole new way of releasing emotional memories. Even in the first few minutes after you try it, you are likely to find the intensity of your traumatic recollections rapidly dropping. There are many scientific studies of EFT for depression, anxiety, and other psychological problems. They show that people who use EFT recover very quickly, often in just a few sessions.

The place that the effectiveness of EFT has been shown most dramatically is in the treatment of post-traumatic stress disorder or PTSD. Thousands of soldiers returning from the battlefields of Iraq and Afghanistan with PTSD have been treated with EFT. Studies have shown that their PTSD symptoms rapidly diminish, as the intensity of those traumatic combat memories drops away.

Not only can EFT improve psychological problems, it can improve physical symptoms too. How is that possible?

There is a strong association between emotional stress and disease. A study of 17,421 adults performed by a hospital chain, Kaiser Permanente, and the Centers for Disease Control and Prevention (CDC) looked at the relationship between their adverse childhood experiences (ACE) and disease (Felitti et al., 1998). ACEs were events like the divorce of their parents, an incarcerated parent, or an addicted parent. The ACE study found that those who had the highest amount of emotional trauma as children had higher rates of many diseases as adults. Those diseases included cancer, heart disease, high blood pressure, obesity, and diabetes. The authors of the study likened the medical establishment to fire fighters who direct all their water at the smoke (physical disease), while ignoring the flames underneath (unresolved emotional trauma).

That's not to say that physical disease is entirely psychological in origin. What it does indicate is that a lifetime of carrying the burden of trauma takes a toll on our bodies. When people use EFT for physical problems, they are releasing the emotional memories associated with the symptom. Once those memories don't hurt anymore, the stress response is reduced, and the body has a chance to heal.

EFT has also been used for sports performance, school performance, and business performance. When the anxieties that claim a large part of people's attention are removed, their full capacities come to bear on the task at hand. That's why you'll find so many stories of athletes and scholars performing better after EFT. There are also specialty books on these subjects, such as *EFT for Sports Performance, EFT for Back Pain, EFT for PTSD, EFT for Weight Loss, EFT for the Highly Sensitive Temperament,* and others.

EFT is easy to learn, and simple to apply. It's so simple that the entire set of instructions fit on a single page, which you'll find later in this chapter. You simply measure the intensity of your emotion associated with a traumatic memory, then pair your memory with a statement of self-acceptance. This pairing utilizes two very well-researched psychological techniques called exposure (remembering the trauma) and cognitive restructuring (self-acceptance). Then, you tap with your fingertips on a series of acupressure points on your face and body. The tapping sends a calming signal to your brain, telling it that you're safe. Whereas before, the memory might send your body into a conditioned stress response, you're now re-conditioning your brain with a positive association. The signal of safety sent by your fingertips tells your brain's stress machinery to disengage. So the conditioned association of the memory with the stress response is broken. Once that loop is broken, it usually stays broken. So later on, when you think of the memory, you no longer feel stressed. It's that easy, and it takes just a minute or two to complete each set of tapping points.

You can then reassess how intensely you react when you think of the memory. If you still get stressed, you do EFT again. People usually find their stress melts like ice cream in the sun. To find out, try it yourself.

EFT draws on principles developed by many of the psychological giants of the last century. The Russian scientist Ivan Pavlov first demonstrated the *conditioned response* in dogs, and the famous American psychologist B. F. Skinner broke conditioning down into smaller packages (called aspects in EFT). Just after World War II, an influential South African psychiatrist, Joseph Wolpe, developed the *stress scale* now used in EFT. The psychologist Aaron Beck discovered that replacing dysfunctional beliefs *(cognitions)* could help people heal from a variety of psychological problems. And exposure therapy (in EFT, remembering the problem) has been shown in many studies to be effective.

The other stream of experience on which EFT draws is Eastern medicine, in the form of acupuncture points (acupoints, for short). Acupuncture has demonstrated efficacy for PTSD and psychological problems, as well as physical ones. Studies have shown that *pressure* on acupuncture points can be as effective as inserting needles, and scientists have also shown that real acupuncture points are more effective than inserting needles into non-acupoints. So EFT is sometimes called "acupuncture without needles," even though it has as much historical basis in Western psychological science as Eastern medicine.

The two streams were brought together in the 1970s when an American psychologist, Roger Callahan, discovered that his patients could be cured of phobias in a single session. To this day, phobias are one of the easiest conditions for EFT to treat. Callahan's system was simplified by Stanford-trained engineer Gary Craig, and gained widespread popularity. EFT has been validated as an evidence-based medicine approach in many studies, including randomized controlled trials that measure PTSD, pain, depression, anxiety, and cravings. EFT is part of a group of therapies called *energy psychology,* because they are believed to affect the body's electromagnetic energy fields.

Here are a couple of stories from the EFTUniverse website, to give you an idea of how EFT is used. The first is from Dr. El March:

> Being in the field of Orthomolecular Medicine for many years, when Ed came to me for lower back pain, we did a variety of things to have him up and running after 3 months of not being able to go to work or do any movements.
>
> I sent him to chiropractors, made him do exercises and did mega vitamin therapy, only to have him back—in the beginning, every few months and, later, every few years. This year Ed came back with the same nagging pain after having the pain on and off and not so severely for about 3 years. He came to my office in great pain and completely stiff, looking for more exercises and advice to ease the situation. This

time I decided to try the EFT method on him and with his permission we started.

I knew that he has been suffering from this for more than 10 years. I first just did three rounds of tapping with him on the pain. The pain went down from a 10 to 5 and back up to 10 again. Then we started talking and I found out that he had been laid off from his job a couple of years back, was in business for himself, and could not afford to take the time off. So we tapped for: *Even though this pain is the only way that I can rest and spend some time at home without feeling guilty that I'm not making an income...*

We also tapped on: *Even though I don't believe this system is going to do anything for me...*

During these tappings, the pain dropped down to an 8 and no matter how many more rounds we did, it kept on going back and forth between 5 and 8.

Then I asked Ed to explain his emotions on the pain and he said, "anger." I asked for further explanation and he went on to tell me the story of how this back pain had come about.

"I was employed at a financial institution as a senior computer center analyst. On the day this happened, I was monitoring the progress on one of the jobs I had given one of my staff to do when we had some computers delivered to our laboratory. As I was looking for someone to set the computers up, my manager, Dan, walked in and asked me to haul the computers to a different location in the lab where they would be waiting for installation.

"I felt his action was uncalled for and disrespectful to my seniority and grade level. This was completely out of line and this was not part of my functions and I felt belittled in front of my direct reports. As I was lifting one of the boxes, the muscle in my back made a noise and I felt a heat rushing through my lower back and then I could not move anymore. I was sent home and stayed on short-term disability for about 3 months and I came to see you 1 month before my recovery to go back to work."

With this explanation, I decided to tap on the feelings he had going back to 1994 and his manager's actions:

Even though my manager was disrespectful to me and belittled me in front of my direct reports and I don't believe he had the right to ask me to do what he did, I completely and lovingly accept myself, I love and respect myself, I forgive myself, and I forgive Dan.

Once we finished tapping on this, the pain dropped from an 8 to 3. Ed kept on calling Dan an "ass," so I did another round of tapping on:

Even though Dan behaved like a complete ass and was completely out of line for asking me to move the computers, I completely and lovingly accept myself. I love and forgive myself and I forgive Dan.

Two rounds of this and Ed's pain was completely gone. He was amazed but did not believe it would last. He went home and I touched base with him the next day and then the next week and a couple of months later — still no pain.

I think this method has added quite an edge to my regular practices and in the meantime I have used it on myself and family members for variety of quick therapies from shoulder pain to headaches, nausea, and so on. This method is absolutely invaluable.

* * *

The second story is about depression, and comes from EFT practitioner Cacina Spaeth:

Recently, I got a new client (I'll call him "Michael"). Michael is a scientist, a total skeptic. He doesn't believe in anything — no energy work, no purpose in life, let alone spirit or anything of that sort. He only came to see me, because 1) a very good girlfriend of his had tried this "tapping thing" and to his surprise actually got better, and 2) because he was desperate enough to try even weird stuff like EFT.

His severe depression simply didn't get any better. On the contrary: Despite the stronger and stronger medication that his psychiatrist kept prescribing him, Michael was less and less able to go to work and clearly caught in a downward spiral regarding his life.

Just for the records: I am no doctor or anything of that sort. I simply use EFT in my coaching practice, teaching people how to use EFT effectively for themselves. Michael was aware of that, and kept taking both his strong antidepressants and sleeping pills as prescribed. In a way, he simply added our EFT sessions to the life he was leading at the time.

As it was such a challenge for Michael to sit with me and try "this whole energy thing," I chose unthreatening and creative wording for our first EFT rounds. He was loosening up significantly. And already after our two sessions he left saying: "This is not therapy. This is *fun!*"

A few weeks later, Michael was oozing joy. When I saw him recently, he was genuinely pissed about his relationship situation. He's had relationships on and off, but it has never worked out. And in his "pissedness," he was spitting out his frustration and sadness about his situation. He's not a loner by choice. After some time, I introduced the idea to him (the physicist!) that—whether we want to acknowledge it or not—we truly do attract a reality that reflects how we resonate. And if we're loaded with the hurts and disenchantments of the past, no wonder we either attract more of the same or no new partner at all.

And then I tapped with him on "potential and probability." Despite what the statistics say, there had to be a woman out there that he would love to be with, and who would feel the same for him. And she wouldn't have to be born first; she was most likely long since around!

Only two days after our "potential" tapping, an attractive woman approached him at work—out of thin air! In the meantime, they e-mailed, they talked, they met, and they even share their love for music. No compromise in sight whatsoever. When Michael came to his most recent session, he said with the brightest smile: "I'm deliriously happy. I'm still pinching myself. And you know what? Even if it wouldn't go on, even if it wouldn't work out with her, it would still be okay for me. Because what happened since last week was already worth it!" And getting a bit more serious, he added: "You know…I used to not believe in stuff like this. But now…. This is too big. This is no coincidence…. It feels strange for me to say this, but I might have become a believer."

"Converting" a scientist simply because what we do works. I love it.

* * *

In a follow-up Cacina Spaeth did on this scientist 4 months later, she found out that he had been able to taper off his depression medication, and eventually eliminated it altogether.

Many scientific studies that measure EFT's effects have been published in peer-reviewed professional journals. There are also several academic papers describing EFT's mechanisms of action, as it affects the brain, nervous system, stress genes, neurotransmitters such as serotonin and dopamine, and stress hormones such as cortisol. You will find them on the research page at EFTUniverse. com. So EFT is supported not just by heart-warming stories, but by a solid base of medical evidence.

EFTUniverse.com is the depository of all the case histories, articles, and tutorials written by the thousands of members of the EFT community worldwide. The e-book *The EFT Mini-Manual* (reprinted here) offers a brief introductory experience of EFT. It gives you enough information to try EFT for yourself. You are encouraged to move on to *The EFT Manual* (Church, 2013), and the specialized books on EFT. You will find thousands of case histories at EFTUniverse.com. The site is fully searchable. You will also find EFT practitioners, training, certification, volunteering opportunities, and many other options on this vast website.

Use the summary sheet "EFT on a Page" later in this chapter to try EFT yourself. The chances are you'll quickly have a positive experience. Give yourself the gift of emotional freedom, and see how quickly both your mind and your body respond!

EFT's Basic Recipe

Over the past decade, EFT has been the focus of a great deal of research. This has resulted in more than 20 clinical trials, in which EFT has been demonstrated to reduce a wide variety of symptoms. These include pain, skin rashes, fibromyalgia, depression, anxiety, and post-traumatic stress disorder (PTSD). Most of these studies have used the standardized form of EFT found in *The EFT Manual.* In this chapter, my goal is to show you how to unlock EFT's healing benefits from whatever physical or psychological problems you're facing. I have a passionate interest in relieving human suffering. When you study EFT, you quickly realize how much suffering can be alleviated with the help of this extraordinary healing tool. I'd like to place the full power of that tool in your hands, so that you can live the happiest, healthiest, and most abundant life possible.

If you go on YouTube or do a Google search, you will find thousands of websites and videos about EFT. The quality of the EFT information you'll find through these sources varies widely, however. Certified practitioners trained in EFT provide a small portion of the information. Most of it consists of personal testimonials by untrained enthusiasts. It's great that EFT works to some degree for virtually anyone. To get the most out of EFT and unlock its full potential, however, it's essential that you learn the form of EFT that's been proven in so many clinical trials. We call this Clinical EFT.

Every year in EFT Universe workshops, we get many people who tell us variations of the same story: "I saw a video on YouTube, tapped along, and got amazing results the first few times. Then it seemed to stop working." The reason for this is that a superficial application of EFT can indeed work wonders. To unleash the full power of EFT, however, requires learning the standardized form we call Clinical EFT, which has been validated, over and over again, by high-quality research, and is taught systematically, step by step, by top experts, in EFT workshops.

Why is EFT able to affect so many problems, both psychological and physical? The reason for its effectiveness is that it reduces stress, and stress is a component of many problems. In EFT research on pain, for instance, we find that pain decreases by an average of 68% with EFT. That's a two-thirds drop, and seems very impressive. Now ask yourself, if EFT can produce a two-thirds drop in pain, why can't it produce a 100% drop? I pondered this question myself, and I asked many therapists and doctors for their theories as to why this might be so.

The consensus is that the two-thirds of pain reduced by EFT is due largely to emotional causes, while the remaining one-third of the pain has a physical derivation. A man I'll call "John" volunteered for a demonstration at an EFT introductory evening at which I presented. He was on crutches, and told us he had a broken leg as a result of a car accident. On a scale of 0 to 10, with 0 being no pain, and 10 being maximum pain, he rated his pain as an 8. The accident had occurred 2 weeks earlier. My logical scientific brain didn't think EFT would work for John, because his pain was purely physical. I tapped with him anyway. At the end of our session, which lasted less than 15 minutes, his pain was down to a 2. I hadn't tapped on the actual pain with John at all, but rather on all the emotional components of the auto accident.

There were many such components. His wife had urged him to drive to an event, but he didn't want to go. He had resentment toward his wife. That's emotional. He was angry at the driver of the other car. That's emotional. He was mad at himself for abandoning his own needs by driving to an event he didn't want to attend. That's emotional. He was upset that now, as an adult, he was reenacting the abandonment he experienced by his mother when he was a child. That's emotional. He was still hurt by an incident that occurred when he was 5 years old, when his mother was supposed to pick him up from a friend's birthday party and forgot because she was socializing with her friends and drinking. That's emotional.

Do you see the pattern here? We're working on a host of problems that are emotional, yet interwoven with the pain. The physical pain is overlaid with a matrix of emotional issues, such as self-neglect, abandonment, anger, and frustration, which are part of the entire fabric of John's life.

The story has a happy ending. After we'd tapped on each of these emotional components of John's pain, the physical pain in his broken leg went down to a 2. That pain rating revealed the extent of the physical component of John's problem. It was a 2. The other six points were emotional.

The same is true for the person who's afraid of public speaking, who has a spider phobia, who's suffering from a physical ailment, who's feeling trapped in his job, who's unhappy with her husband, who's in conflict with those around him. All of these problems have a large component of unfinished emotional business from the past. When you neutralize the underlying emotional issues with EFT, what remains is the real problem, which is often far smaller than you imagine.

Though I present at few conferences nowadays because of other demands on my time, I used to present at about 30 medical and psychological conferences each year, speaking about research and teaching EFT. I presented to thousands of medical professionals during that period. One of my favorite sayings was "Don't medicalize emotional problems. And don't emotionalize medical problems." When I would say this to a roomful of physicians, they would nod their heads in unison. The medical profession as a whole is very aware of the emotional component of disease.

If you have a real medical problem, you need good medical care. No ifs, ands, or buts. If you have an emotional problem, you need EFT. Most problems are a mixture of both. That's why I urge you to work on the emotional component with EFT and other safe and noninvasive behavioral methods, and to get the best possible medical care for the physical component of your problem. Talk to your doctor about this; virtually every physician will be supportive of you bolstering your medical treatment with emotional catharsis.

When you feel better emotionally, a host of positive changes also occur in your energy system. When you feel worse, your energy system follows. Several researchers have hooked people up to electroencephalographs (EEGs), and taken EEG readings of the electrical energy in their brains before and after EFT. These studies show that when subjects are asked to recall a traumatic event, their patterns of brain-wave activity change. The brain-wave frequencies associated with stress, and activation of the fight-or-flight response, dominate their EEG readings. After successful treatment, the brain waves shown on their EEG readings are those that characterize relaxation.

Other research has shown similar results from acupuncture. The theory behind acupuncture is that our body's energy flows in 12 channels called meridians.

When that energy is blocked, physical or psychological distress occurs. The use of acupuncture needles, or acupressure with the fingertips, is believed to release those energy blocks. EFT has you tap with your fingertips on the end points of those meridians; that's why it's sometimes called "emotional acupuncture." When your energy is balanced and flowing, whether it's the brain-wave energy picked up by the EEG or the meridian energy described in acupuncture, you feel better. That's another reason why EFT works well for many different kinds of problem.

EFT is rooted in sound science, and this chapter is devoted to showing you how to do Clinical EFT yourself. It will introduce you to the basic concepts that amplify the power of EFT, and steer you clear of the most common pitfalls that prevent people from making progress with EFT. The basics of EFT are easy to use and quick to learn. We call this EFT's "Basic Recipe." The second half of this chapter shows you how to apply the Basic Recipe for maximum effect. It introduces you to all of the concepts key to Clinical EFT.

Testing

EFT doesn't just hope to be effective. We test our results constantly, to determine if the course we're taking is truly making us feel better. The basic scale we use for testing was developed by a famous psychiatrist called Joseph Wolpe in the 1950s, and measures our degree of discomfort on a scale of 0 through 10. Zero indicates no discomfort, and 10 is the maximum possible distress. This scale works equally well for psychological problems such as anxiety and physical problems such as pain.

Dr. Wolpe called this rating SUD or Subjective Units of Discomfort. It's also sometimes called Subjective Units of Distress. You feel your problem, and give it a number on the SUD scale. It's vital to rate your SUD level as it is *right now,* not imagine what it might have been at the time in the past when the traumatic event occurred. If you can't quickly identify a number, just take your best guess, and go from there.

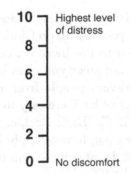

SUD scale (intensity meter)

I recommend you write down your initial SUD number. It's also worth noting *where in your body* the information on your SUD level is coming from. If you're working on a physical pain such as a headache, where in your head is the ache centered? If you're working on a traumatic emotional event, perhaps a car accident, where in your body is your reference point for your emotional distress? Do you feel it in your belly, your heart, your forehead? Write down the location on which your SUD is based.

A variation of the numeric scale is a visual scale. For example, if you're working with a child who does not yet know how to count, you can ask the child to spread his or her hands apart to indicate how big the problem is. Wide-open arms means big, and hands close together means small.

Whatever means you use to test, each round of EFT tapping usually begins with this type of assessment of the size of the problem. This allows us to determine whether or not our approach is working. After we've tested and written down our SUD level and body location, we move on to EFT's Basic Recipe. It has this name to indicate that EFT consists of certain ingredients, and if you want to be successful, you need to include them, just the way you need to include all the ingredients in a recipe for chocolate chip cookies if you want your end product to be tasty.

Many years ago I published a book by Wally Amos. Wally is better known as "Famous Amos" for his brand of chocolate chip cookies. One day I asked Wally, "Where did you get your recipe?" I thought he was going to tell me how he'd experimented with hundreds of variations to find the best possible combination of ingredients. I imagined Wally like Thomas Edison in his laboratory, obsessively combining pinches of this and smidgeons of that, year after year, in order to perfect the flavor of his cookies, the way Edison tried thousands of combinations before discovering the incandescent light bulb.

Wally's offhand response was, "I used the recipe on the back of a pack of Toll House chocolate chips." Toll House is one of the most popular brands, selling millions of packages each year, and the simple recipe is available to everyone. I was astonished, and laughed at how different the reality was from my imaginary picture of Wally as Edison. Yet the message is simple: Don't reinvent the wheel. If it works, it works. Toll House is so popular because their recipe works. Clinical EFT produces such good results because the Basic Recipe works. While a master chef might be experienced enough to produce exquisite variations, a beginner can bake excellent cookies, and get consistently great results, just by following the basic recipe. This chapter is designed to provide you with that simple yet reliable level of knowledge.

EFT's Basic Recipe omits a procedure that was part of the earliest forms of EFT, called the 9 Gamut Procedure. Though the 9 Gamut Procedure has great value for certain conditions, it isn't always necessary, so we leave it out. The version of EFT that includes it is called the Full Basic Recipe (see Appendix A of *The EFT Manual*).

The Setup Statement

The Setup Statement systematically "sets up" the problem you want to work on. Think about arranging dominoes in a line in the game of creating a chain reaction. Before you start the game, you set them up. The object of the game is to knock them down, just the way EFT expects to knock down your SUD level, but to start with, you set up the pieces of the problem.

The Setup Statement has its roots in two schools of psychology. One is called cognitive therapy, and the other is called exposure therapy. Cognitive therapy considers the large realm of your cognitions—your thoughts, beliefs, ways of relating to others, and the mental frames through which you perceive the world and your experiences.

Exposure therapy is a successful branch of psychotherapy that vividly exposes you to your negative experiences. Rather than avoiding them, you're confronted by them, with the goal of breaking your conditioned fear response to the event.

We won't go deeper into these two forms of therapy now, but you'll later see how EFT's Setup Statement draws from cognitive and exposure approaches to form a powerful combination with acupressure or tapping.

Psychological Reversal

The term Psychological Reversal is taken from energy therapies. It refers to the concept that when your energies are blocked or reversed, you develop symptoms. If you put the batteries into a flashlight backward, with the positive end where the negative should be, the light won't shine. The human body also has a polarity (see illustration). A reversal of normal polarity will block the flow of energy through the body. In acupuncture, the goal of treatment is to remove obstructions, and to allow the free flow of energy through the 12 meridians. If reversal occurs, it impedes the healing process.

The way Psychological Reversal shows up in EFT and other energy therapies is as a failure to make progress in resolving the problem. It's especially prevalent in chronic diseases, addictions, and conditions that resist healing. If you run into a person who's desperate to recover, yet who has had no success even with a wide variety of different therapies, the chances are good that you're dealing with

Psychological Reversal. One of the first steps of EFT's Basic Recipe is to correct for Psychological Reversal. It only takes a few seconds, so we include this step whether or not Psychological Reversal is present.

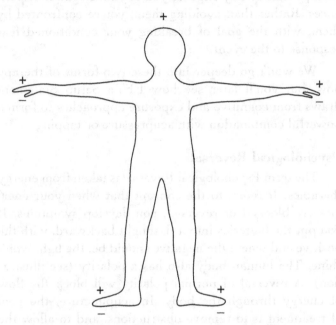

The human body's electrical polarity (adapted from
ACEP Certification Program Manual, 2006)

EFT's Setup includes stating an affirmation with those elements drawn from cognitive and exposure therapies, while at the same time correcting for Psychological Reversal.

Affirmation

The exposure part of the Setup Statement involves remembering the problem. You expose your mind repeatedly to the memory of the trauma. This is the opposite of what we normally do; we usually want an emotional trauma to fade away. We might engage in behaviors like dissociation or avoidance so that we don't have to deal with unpleasant memories.

As you gain confidence with EFT, you'll find yourself becoming fearless when it comes to exposure. You'll discover you don't have to remain afraid of old traumatic memories; you have a tool that allows you to reduce their emotional intensity in minutes or even seconds. The usual pattern of running away from a problem is reversed. You feel confident running toward it, knowing that you'll quickly feel better.

The EFT Setup Statement is this: *Even though I have (name of problem), I deeply and completely accept myself.*

You insert the name of the problem in the exposure half of the Setup Statement. Examples might be:

Even though I had that dreadful car crash, I deeply and completely accept myself.

Even though I have this migraine headache, I deeply and completely accept myself.

Even though I have this fear of heights, I deeply and completely accept myself.

Even though I have this pain in my knees, I deeply and completely accept myself.

Even though I had my buddy die in my arms in Iraq, I deeply and completely accept myself.

Even though I have this huge craving for whiskey, I deeply and completely accept myself.

Even though I have this fear of spiders, I deeply and completely accept myself.

Even though I have this urge to eat another cookie, I deeply and completely accept myself.

The list of variations is infinite. You can use this Setup Statement for anything that bothers you.

While exposure is represented by the first half of the Setup Statement, before the comma, cognitive work is done by the second half of the statement, the part that deals with self-acceptance. EFT doesn't try to induce you to positive thinking. You don't tell yourself that things will get better, or that you'll improve. You simply express the intention of accepting yourself just the way you are. You accept reality. Gestalt therapist Byron Katie wrote a book entitled *Loving What Is*, and that's exactly what EFT recommends you do.

The Serenity Prayer uses the same formula of acceptance, with the words, "God grant me the serenity to accept the things I cannot change; courage to change the things I can; and wisdom to know the difference." With EFT you don't try and think positively. You don't try and change your attitude or circumstances; you simply affirm that you accept them. This cognitive frame of accepting what is opens the path to change in a profound way. It's also quite difficult to do this in our culture, which bombards us with positive thinking. Positive thinking actually gets in the way of healing in many cases, while acceptance provides us with a reality-based starting point congruent with our experience. The great 20th-century therapist Carl Rogers, who introduced client-centered therapy, said that the paradox of transformation is that change begins by accepting conditions exactly the way they are.

I recommend that you use the Setup Statement in exactly this way at first, but as you gain confidence, you can experiment with different variations. The only requirement is that you include both a self-acceptance statement and exposure to the problem. For instance, you can invert the two halves of the formula, and put cognitive self-acceptance first, followed by exposure. Here are some examples:

I accept myself fully and completely, even with this miserable headache.

I deeply love myself, even though I have nightmares from that terrible car crash.

I hold myself in high esteem, even though I feel such pain from my divorce.

When you're doing EFT with children, you don't need an elaborate Setup Statement. You can have children use very simple self-acceptance phrases, like "I'm okay" or "I'm a great kid." Such a Setup Statement might look like this:

Even though Johnny hit me, I'm okay.

The teacher was mean to me, but I'm still an amazing kid.

You'll be surprised how quickly children respond to EFT. Their SUD levels usually drop so fast that adults have a difficult time accepting the shift. Although we haven't yet done the research to discover why children are so receptive to change, my hypothesis is that their behaviors haven't yet been cemented by years of conditioning. They've not yet woven a thick neural grid in their brains through repetitive thinking and behavior, so they can let go of negative emotions fast.

What do you do if your problem is self-acceptance itself? What if you believe you're unacceptable? What if you have low self-esteem, and the words "I deeply and completely accept myself" sound like a lie?

What EFT suggests you do in such a case is say the words anyway, even if you don't believe them. They will usually have some effect, even if at first you have difficulty with them. As you correct for Psychological Reversal in the way I will show you here, you will soon find yourself shifting from unbelief to belief that you are acceptable. You can say the affirmation aloud or silently. It carries more emotional energy if it is said emphatically or loudly, and imagined vividly.

Secondary Gain

While energy therapies use the term "psychological reversal" to indicate energy blocks to healing, there's an equivalent term drawn from psychology. That term is "secondary gain." It refers to the benefits of being sick. "Why would anyone want to be sick?" you might wonder. There are actually many reasons for keeping a mental or physical problem firmly in place.

Consider the case of a veteran with PTSD. He's suffering from flashbacks of scenes from Afghanistan where he witnessed death and suffering. He has nightmares, and never sleeps through the night. He's so disturbed that he cannot hold down a job or keep a relationship intact for long. Why would such a person not want to get better, considering the damage PTSD is doing to his life?

The reason might be that he's getting a disability check each month as a result of his condition. His income is dependent on having PTSD, and if he recovers, his main source of livelihood might disappear with it.

Another reason might be that he was deeply wounded by a divorce many years ago. He lost his house and children in the process. He's fearful of getting into another romantic relationship that is likely to end badly. PTSD gives him a reason to not try.

These are obvious examples of secondary gain. When we work with participants in EFT workshops, we uncover a wide variety of subtle reasons that stand in the way of healing. One woman had been trying to lose weight for 5 years and had failed at every diet she tried. Her secondary gain turned out to be freedom from unwanted attention by men.

Another woman, this time with fibromyalgia, discovered that her secret benefit from the disease was that she didn't have to visit relatives she didn't like. She had a ready excuse for avoiding social obligations. She also got sympathetic attention from her husband and children for her suffering. If she gave up her painful disease, she might lose a degree of affection from her family and have to resume seeing the relatives she detested.

Just like Psychological Reversal, secondary gain prevents us from making progress on our healing journey. Correcting for these hidden obstacles to success is one of the first elements in EFT's Basic Recipe.

How EFT Corrects for Psychological Reversal

The first tapping point we use in the EFT routine is called the Karate Chop point, because it's located on the fleshy outer portion of the hand, the part used in karate to deliver a blow. EFT has you tap the Karate Chop point with the tips of the other four fingers of the opposite hand.

The Karate Chop (KC) Point

Repeat your affirmation emphatically three times while tapping your Karate Chop point. You've now corrected for psychological reversal, and set up your energy system for the next part of EFT's Basic Recipe, the Sequence.

The Sequence

You now tap on meridian end points in sequence. Tap firmly, but not harshly, with the tips of your first two fingers, about seven times on each point. The exact number is not important; it can be a few more or less than seven. You can tap on either the right or left side of your body, with either your dominant or nondominant hand.

First tap on the meridian end points found on the face. These are: (1) at the start of the eyebrow, where it joins the bridge of the nose; (2) on the outside edge of the eye socket; (3) on the bony ridge of the eye socket under the pupil; (4) under the nose; and (5) between the lower lip and the chin.

EB, SE, UE, UN and Ch Points

Then tap (6) on one of the collarbone points (see illustration). To locate this point, place a finger in the notch between your collarbones. Move your finger down about an inch and you'll feel a hollow in your breastbone. Now move it to the side about an inch and you'll find a deep hollow below your collarbone. You've now located the collarbone acupressure point.

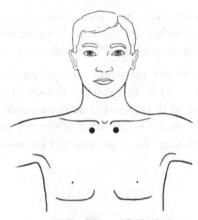

The Collarbone (CB) Points

About four inches below the armpit (for women, this is where a bra strap crosses), you'll find (7) the under the arm point.

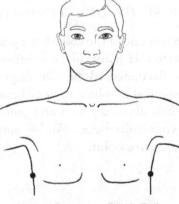

Under the Arm (UA) Points

The Reminder Phrase

Earlier, I emphasized the importance of exposure. Exposure therapy has been the subject of much research, which has shown that prolonged exposure to a problem, when coupled with techniques to calm the body, effectively treats traumatic stress. EFT incorporates exposure in the form of a Reminder Phrase. This is a brief phrase that keeps the problem at the front of your mind while you tap on the acupressure points. It keeps your energy system focused on the specific issue you're working on, rather than jumping to other thoughts and feelings. The aim of the Reminder Phrase is to bring the problem vividly into your experience, even though the emotionally triggering situation might not be present now.

For instance, if you have test anxiety, you use the Reminder Phrase to keep you focused on the fear, even though you aren't actually taking a test right now. That gives EFT an opportunity to shift the pattern in the absence of the real problem. You can also use EFT during an actual situation, such as when you're taking an actual test, but most of the time you're working on troublesome memories. The Reminder Phrase keeps you targeted on the problem. An example of a Reminder Phrase for test anxiety might be *"That test"* or *"The test I have to take tomorrow"* or *"That test I failed."* Other examples of Reminder Phrases are:

> *The beesting*
> *Dad hit me*
> *Friend doesn't respect me*

Lawyer's office
Sister told me I was fat
Car crash
This knee pain

Tap each point while repeating your Reminder Phrase. Then tune in to the problem again, and get a second SUD rating. The chances are good that your SUD score will now be much lower than it was before. These instructions might seem complicated the first time you read them, but you'll soon find you're able to complete a round of EFT tapping from memory in one to two minutes.

Let's now summarize the steps of EFT's Basic Recipe.

1. Assess your SUD level.

2. Insert the name of your problem into the Setup Statement: *"Even though I have (this problem), I deeply and completely accept myself."*

3. Tap continuously on the Karate Chop point while repeating the Setup Statement three times.

4. While repeating the Reminder Phrase, tap about seven times on the other seven points.

5. Test your results with a second SUD rating.

Isn't that simple? You now have a tool that, in just a minute or two, can effectively neutralize the emotional sting of old memories, as well as help you get through bad current situations. After a few rounds of tapping, you'll find you've effortlessly memorized the Basic Recipe, and you'll find yourself using it often in your daily life

If Your SUD Level Doesn't Come Down to 0

Sometimes a single round of tapping brings your SUD score to 0. Sometimes it only brings it down slightly. Your migraine might have been an 8, and after a round of EFT it's a 4. In these cases, we do EFT again. You can adjust your affirmation to acknowledge that a portion of the problem sill remains, for example, *"Even though I still have some of this migraine, I deeply and completely accept myself."* Hear are some further examples:

> *Even though I still feel some anger toward my friend for putting me down, I deeply and completely accept myself.*

> *Even though I still have a little twinge of that knee pain, I deeply and completely accept myself.*

> *Even though the beesting still smarts slightly, I deeply and completely accept myself.*

> *Even though I'm still harboring some resentment toward my boss, I deeply and completely accept myself.*

> *Even though I'm still somewhat frustrated with my daughter for breaking her agreement, I deeply and completely accept myself.*

> *Even though I'm still upset when I think of being shipped to Iraq, I deeply and completely accept myself.*

Adjust the Reminder Phrase accordingly, as in *"some anger still"* or *"remaining frustration"* or *"bit of pain"* or *"somewhat upset."*

EFT for You and Others

You can do EFT on yourself, as you've experienced during these practice rounds. You can also tap on others. Many therapists, life coaches, and other practitioners offer EFT professionally to clients. Personally, I'm far more inclined to have clients tap on themselves during EFT sessions, even during the course of a therapy or coaching session. Though the coach can tap on the client, having the client tap on themselves, along with some guidance by the coach, puts the power squarely in the hands of the client. The client is empowered by discovering that they are able to reduce their own emotional distress, and leaves the coaches office with a self-help tool at their fingertips any time they need it. In some jurisdictions, it is illegal or unethical for therapists to touch clients at all, and EFT when done only by the client is still effective in these cases.

The Importance of Targeting Specific Events

During EFT workshops, I sometimes write on the board:

The Three Most Important Things About EFT

Then, under that, I write:

Specific Events

Specific Events

Specific Events

It's my way of driving home the point that a focus on specific events is critical to success in EFT. In order to release old patterns of emotion and behavior, it's vital to identify and correct the specific events that gave rise to those problems. When you hear people say, "I tried EFT and it didn't work," the chances are good that they were tapping on generalities, instead of specifics.

An example of a generality is "self-esteem" or "depression" or "performance problems." These aren't specific events. Beneath these generalities is a collection of specific events. The person with low self-esteem might have been coloring a picture at the age of 4 when her mother walked in and criticized her for drawing outside the lines. She might have had another experience of a schoolteacher scolding her for playing with her hair during class in second grade, and a third experience of her first boyfriend deciding to ask another girl to the school dance. Together, those specific events contribute to the global pattern of low self-esteem. The way EFT works is that when the emotional trauma of those individual events is resolved, the whole pattern of low self-esteem can shift. If you tap on the big pattern, and omit the specific events, you're likely to have limited success.

When you think about how a big pattern like low self-esteem is established, this makes sense. It's built up out of many single events. Collectively, they form the whole pattern. The big pattern doesn't spring to life fully formed; it's built up gradually out of many similar experiences. The memories engraved in your brain are of individual events; one disappointing or traumatic memory at a time is encoded in your memory bank. When enough similar memories have accumulated, their commonalities combine to create a common theme like "poor self-esteem." Yet the theme originated as a series of specific events, and that's where EFT can be effectively applied.

You don't have to use EFT on every single event that contributed to the global theme. Usually, once a few of the most disturbing memories have lost their emotional impact, the whole pattern disappears. Memories that are similar lose their impact once the most vivid memories have been neutralized with EFT.

Tapping on global issues is the single most common mistake newcomers make with EFT. Using lists of tapping phrases from a website or a book, or tapping on generalities, is far less effective than tuning into the events that contributed to your global problem, and tapping on them. If you hear someone say, "EFT doesn't work," the chances are good they've been tapping globally rather than identifying specific events. Don't make this elementary mistake. List the events, one after the other, that stand out most vividly in your mind when you think about the global problem. Tap on each of them, and you'll usually find the global problem diminishing of its own accord. This is called the "generalization effect," and it's one of the key concepts in EFT.

Tapping on Aspects

EFT breaks traumatic events and other problems into smaller pieces called aspects. The reason for this is that the highest emotional charge is typically found in one small chunk of the event, rather than the entirety of the event. You might need to identify several different aspects, and tap on each of them, before the intensity of the whole event is reduced to a 0.

Here's an example of tapping on aspects, drawn from experience at an EFT workshop I taught. A woman in her late 30s volunteered as a subject. She'd had neck pain and limited range of motion since an automobile accident 6 years before. She could turn her head to the right most of the way but had only a few degrees of movement to the left. The accident had been a minor one, and why she still suffered 6 years later was something of a mystery to her.

I asked her to feel where in her body she felt the most intensity when recalling the accident, and she said it was in her upper chest. I then asked her about the first time she'd ever felt that way, and she said it was when she'd been involved in another auto accident at the age of 8. Her sister had been driving the car. We worked on each aspect of the early accident. The two girls had hit another car head on at low speed while driving around a bend on a country road. One emotionally triggering aspect was the moment she realized that a collision was unavoidable, and we tapped till that lost its force. We tapped on the sound of the crash, another aspect. She had been taken to a neighbor's house, bleeding from a cut on her head, and we tapped on that. We tapped on aspect after aspect. Still, her pain level didn't go down much, and her range of motion didn't improve.

Then she gasped and said, "I just remembered. My sister was only 15 years old. She was underage. That day, I dared her to drive the family car, and we totaled it." Her guilt turned out to be the aspect that held the most emotional charge, and after we tapped on that, her pain disappeared, and she regained full range of motion in her neck. If we'd tapped on the later accident, or failed to uncover all the aspects, we might have thought, "EFT doesn't work."

Aspects can be pains, physical sensations, emotions, images, sounds, tastes, odors, fragments of an event, or beliefs. Make sure you dig deep for all the emotional charge held in each aspect of an event before you move on to the next one. One way of doing this is to check each sensory channel, and ask, "What did you hear/see/taste/touch/smell?" For one person, the burned-rubber smell of skidding tires might be the most terrifying aspect of a car accident. For another, it might be the smell of blood. Yet another person might remember most vividly the sound of the crash or the screams. For another person, the maximum emotional charge might be held in the feeling of terror at the moment of realization that the crash is inevitable. The pain itself might be an aspect. Guilt, or any other emotion, can be an aspect. For traumatic events, it's necessary to tap on each aspect.

Thorough exploration of all the aspects will usually yield a complete neutralization of the memory. If there's still some emotional charge left, the chances are good that you've missed an aspect, so go back and find out what shards of trauma might still be stuck in place.

Finding Core Issues

One of my favorite sayings during EFT workshops is "The problem is never the problem." What I mean by this is that the problem we complain about today usually bothers us only because it resembles an earlier problem. For example, if your spouse being late disturbs you, you may discover by digging deep with EFT that the real reason this behavior triggers you is that your mother didn't meet your needs in early childhood. Your spouse's behavior in the present day resembles, to your brain, the neglect you experienced in early childhood, so you react accordingly. You put a lot of energy into trying to change your spouse when the present-day person is not the source of the problem.

On the EFT Universe website, we have published hundreds of stories in which someone was no longer triggered by a present problem after the emotional charge was removed from a similar childhood event. Nothing changed in the present day, yet the very problem that so vexed a person before now carries zero emotional charge. That's the magic that happens once we neutralize core issues with EFT. Rather than being content with using EFT on surface problems, it's worth developing the skills to find and resolve the core issues that are at the root of the problem.

Here are some questions you might ask in order to identify core issues:

- Does the problem that's bothering you remind you of any events in your childhood? Tune into your body and feel your feelings. Then travel back in time to the first time in your life you ever felt that same sensation.

- What's the worst similar experience you ever had?

- If you were writing your autobiography, what chapter would you prefer to delete, as though it had never happened to you?

If you can't remember a specific childhood event, simply make up a fictional event in your mind. This kind of guessing usually turns out to be right on target. You're assembling the imagined event out of components of real events, and the imaginary event usually leads back to actual events you can tap on. Even if it doesn't, and you tap on the fictional event, you will usually experience an obvious release of tension.

The Generalization Effect

The *generalization effect* is a phenomenon you'll notice as you make progress with EFT. As you resolve the emotional sting of specific events, other events with a similar emotional signature also decrease in intensity. I once worked with a man at an EFT workshop whose father had beaten him many times during his childhood. His SUD level on the beatings was a 10. I asked him to recall the worst beating he'd ever suffered. He told me that when he was 8 years old, his father had hit him so hard he had broken the boy's jaw. We tapped together on that terrible beating, and after working on all the aspects, his SUD dropped to a 0. I asked him for a SUD score on all the beatings, and his face softened. He said, "My dad got beat by his dad much worse than he beat me. My dad actually did a pretty good job considering how badly he was raised." My client's SUD level on all the beatings dropped considerably after we reduced the intensity of this one beating. That's an example of EFT's generalization effect. When you knock down an important domino, all the other dominos can fall.

This is very reassuring to clients who suffered from many instances of childhood abuse, the way my client at that workshop had suffered. You don't need to work through every single horrible incident. Often, simply collapsing the emotional intensity behind one incident is sufficient to collapse the intensity around similar incidents.

The reason our brains work this way is because of a group of neurons in the emotional center of the brain, the limbic system, called the hippocampus. The hippocampus has the job of comparing one event to the other. Suppose that, as a 5-year-old child in Catholic school, you get beaten by a nun. Forty years later, you can't figure out why you feel uneasy around women wearing outfits that are black and white. The reason for your adult aversion to a black-and-white combination is that the hippocampus associates the colors of the nun's habit with the pain of the beating.

This was a brilliant evolutionary innovation for your ancestors. Perhaps these early humans were attacked by a tiger hiding in the long grass. The tiger's stripes mimicked the patterns of the grass yet there was something different there. Learning to spot a pattern, judge the differences, and react with fear saved your alert ancestors. They gave birth to their children, who also learned, just a little bit better, how to respond to threats. After thousands of generations, you have a hippocampus at the center of your brain that is genetically engineered to evaluate every message flooding in from your senses, and pick out those associated with the possibility of danger. You see the woman wearing the black-and-white cocktail dress at a party, your hippocampus associates these colors with the nun who beat you, and you have an emotional response.

Yet the opposite is also true. Assume for a moment you're a man who is very shy when confronted with women at cocktail parties. He feels a rush of fear whenever he thinks about talking to an attractive woman dressed in black. He works with an EFT coach on his memories of getting beaten by the nun in Catholic school, and suddenly he finds himself able to talk easily to women at parties. Once the man's hippocampus breaks the connection between beatings and a black dress, it knows, for future reference, that the two phenomena are no longer connected.

This is the explanation the latest brain science gives us for the generalization effect. It's been noted in EFT for many years, and it's very comforting for those who've suffered many adverse experiences. You may need to tap on some of them, but you won't have to tap on all of them before the whole group is neutralized. Sometimes, like my client who was beaten repeatedly as a child, if you tap on a big one, the generalization effect reduces the emotional intensity of all similar experiences.

The Movie Technique and Tell the Story Technique

When you take an EFT workshop, the first key technique you learn is the Movie Technique. Why do we place such emphasis on the Movie Technique? The reason for this is that it combines many of the methods that are key to success with EFT.

The first thing the Movie Technique does is focus you on being specific. EFT is great at eliminating the emotional intensity you feel, as long as it's used on an actual concrete event ("John yelled at me in the meeting"), rather than a general statement ("My procrastination").

The Movie Technique has you identify a particular incident that has a big emotional charge for you, and systematically reduce that charge to 0. You picture the event in your mind's eye just as though it were a movie, and run through the movie scene by scene.

Whenever you reach a part of the movie that carries a big emotional charge, you stop and perform the EFT sequence. In this way, you reduce the intensity of each of the bad parts of the movie. EFT's related technique, Tell the Story, is done out loud, while the Movie Technique is typically done silently. You can use the Movie Technique with a client without the client ever disclosing what the event was.

Try this with one of your own traumatic life events right now. Think of the event as though it were a scary movie. Make sure it's an event that lasts just a few minutes; if your movie lasts several hours or days, you've probably picked a general pattern. Try again, selecting a different event, till you have a movie that's just a few minutes long.

One example is a man whose general issue is "Distrust of Strangers." We trace it to a particular childhood incident that occurred when the man, whom we'll call John, was 7 years old. His parents moved to a new town, and John found himself walking to a new school through a rough neighborhood. He encountered a group of bullies at school but always managed to avoid them. One day, walking back from school, he saw the bullies walking toward him. He crossed the street, hoping to avoid their attention. He wasn't successful, and he saw them point at him, then change course to intercept him. He knew he was due for a beating. They taunted him and shoved him, and he fell into the gutter. His mouth hit the pavement, and he chipped a tooth. Other kids gathered round and laughed at him, and the bullies moved off. He picked himself up and walked the rest of the way home.

If you were to apply EFT to John's general pattern, "Distrust of Strangers," you'd be tapping generally—and ineffectually. When instead you focus on the specific event, you're honing in on the life events that gave rise to the general pattern. A collection of events like John's beating can combine to create the general pattern.

Now give your movie a title. John might call his movie "The Bullies."

Start thinking about the movie at a point before the traumatic part began. For John, that would be when he was walking home from school, unaware of the events in store for him.

Now run your movie through your mind till the end. The end of the movie is usually a place where the bad events come to an end. For John, this might be when he picked himself up off the ground, and resumed his walk home.

Now let's add EFT to your movie. Here's the way you do this:

1. Think of the title of your movie. Rate your degree of your emotional distress around just the title, not the movie itself. For instance, on the distress scale of 0 to 10 where 0 is no distress and 10 represents maximum distress, you might be an 8 when you think of the title "The Meeting." Write down your movie title, and your number.

2. Work the movie title into an EFT Setup Statement. It might sound something like this: "Even though I experienced [Insert Your Movie Title Here], I deeply and completely accept myself." Then tap on the EFT acupressure points, while repeating the Setup Statement three times. Your distress level will typically go down. You may have to do EFT several times on the title for it to reach a low number like 0 or 1 or 2.

3. Once the title reaches a low number, think of the "neutral point" before the bad events in the movie began to take place. For John, the neutral point was when he was walking home from school, before the bullies saw him. Once you've identified the neutral point of your own movie, start running the movie through your mind, until you reach a point where the emotional intensity rises. In John's case, the first emotionally intense point was when he saw the bullies.

4. Stop at this point, and assess your intensity number. It might have risen from a 1 to a 7, for instance. Then perform a round of EFT on that first emotional crescendo. For John, it might be, "Even though I saw

the bullies turn toward me, I deeply and completely accept myself." Use the same kind of statement for your own problem: "Even though [first emotional crescendo], I deeply and completely accept myself." Keep tapping till your number drops to 0 or near 0, perhaps a 1 or 2.

5. Now rewind your mental movie to the neutral point, and start running it in your mind again. Stop at the first emotional crescendo. If you sail right through the first one you tapped on, you know you've really and truly resolved that aspect of the memory with EFT. Go on to the next crescendo. For John, this might have been when they shoved him into the gutter. When you've found your second emotional crescendo, then repeat the process. Assess your intensity number, do EFT, and keep tapping till your number is low. Even if your number is only a 3 or 4, stop and do EFT again. Don't push through low-intensity emotional crescendos; since you have the gift of freedom at your fingertips, use it on each part of the movie.

6. Rewind to the neutral point again, and repeat the process.

7. When you can replay the whole movie in your mind, from the neutral point, to the end of the movie when your feelings are neutral again, you'll know you've resolved the whole event. You'll have dealt with all the aspects of the traumatic incident.

8. To truly test yourself, run through the movie, but exaggerate each sensory channel. Imagine the sights, sounds, smells, tastes, and other aspects of the movie

as vividly as you possible can. If you've been running the movie silently in your mind, speak it out loud. When you cannot possibly make yourself upset, you're sure to have resolved the lingering emotional impact of the event. The effect is usually permanent.

When you work through enough individual movies in this way, the whole general pattern often vanishes. Perhaps John had 40 events that contributed to his distrust of strangers. He might need to do the Movie Technique on all 40, but experience with EFT suggests that when you resolve just a few key events, perhaps 5 or 10 of them, the rest fade in intensity, and the general pattern itself is neutralized.

The Tell the Story Technique is similar to the Movie Technique; usually the Movie Technique is performed silently while Tell the Story is out loud. One great benefit of the Movie Technique done silently is that the client does not have to disclose the nature of the problem. An event might be too triggering, or too embarrassing, or too emotionally overwhelming, to be spoken out loud. That's no problem with the Movie Technique, which allows EFT to work its magic without the necessity of disclosure on the part of the client. The privacy offered by the Movie Technique makes it very useful for clients who would rather not talk openly about troubling events.

Constricted Breathing Technique

Here's a way to demonstrate how EFT can affect you physically. You can try this yourself right now. It's also often practiced as an onstage demonstration at EFT workshops. You simply take three deep breaths, stretching your lungs as far as they can expand. On the third breath, rate the extent of the expansion of your lungs on a 0 to 10 scale, with 0 being as constricted as possible, and 10 being as expanded as possible. Now perform several rounds of EFT using Setup Statements such as:

>*Even though my breathing is constricted...*
>
>*Even though my lungs will only expand to an 8...*
>
>*Even though I have this physical problem that prevents me breathing deeply...*

Now take another deep breath and rate your level of expansion. Usually there's substantial improvement. Now focus on any emotional contributors to constricted breathing. Use questions like:

>*What life events can I associate with breathing problems?*
>
>*Are there places in my life where I feel restricted?*
>
>*If I simply guess at an emotional reason for my constricted breathing, what might it be?*

Now tap on any issues surfaced by these questions. After your intensity is reduced, take another deep breath and rate how far your lungs are now expanding. Even if you were a 10 earlier, you might now find you're an 11 or 14.

The Personal Peace Procedure

The Personal Peace Procedure consists of listing every specific troublesome event in your life and systematically using EFT to tap away the emotional impact of these events. With due diligence, you knock over every negative domino on your emotional playing board and, in so doing, remove significant sources of both emotional and physical ailments. You experience personal peace, which improves your work and home relationships, your health, and every other area of your life.

Tapping on large numbers of events one by one might seem like a daunting task, but we'll show you in the next few paragraphs how you can accomplish it quickly and efficiently. Because of EFT's generalization effect, where tapping on one issue reduces the intensity of similar issues, you'll typically find the process going much faster than you imagined.

Removing the emotional charge from your specific events results in less and less internal conflict. Less internal conflict results, in turn, in greater personal peace and less suffering on all levels—physical, mental, emotional, and spiritual. For many people, the Personal Peace Procedure has led to the complete cessation of lifelong issues that other methods did not resolve. You'll find stories on the EFT Universe website written by people who describe relief from physical maladies like headaches, breathing difficulties, and digestive disorders. You'll read other stories of people who used EFT to help them deal with the stress associated with AIDS, multiple sclerosis, and cancer. Unresolved anger, traumas, guilt, or grief contributes to physical illness, and cannot be medicated away. EFT addresses these emotional contributors to physical disease.

Here's how to do the Personal Peace Procedure:

1. List every specific troublesome event in your life that you can remember. Write them down in a Personal Peace Procedure journal. "Troublesome" means it caused you some form of discomfort. If you listed fewer than 50 events, try harder to remember more. Many people find hundreds. Some bad events you recall may not seem to cause you any current discomfort. List them anyway. The fact that they came to mind suggests they may need resolution. As you list them, give each specific event a title, like it's a short movie, such as: Mom slapped me that time in the car; I stole my brother's baseball cap; I slipped and fell in front of everybody at the ice skating rink; My third grade class ridiculed me when I gave that speech; Dad locked me in the toolshed overnight; Mrs. Simmons told me I was dumb.

2. When your list is finished, choose the biggest dominoes on your board, that is, the events that have the most emotional charge for you. Apply EFT to them, one at a time, until the SUD level for each event is 0. You might find yourself laughing about an event that used to bring you to tears; you might find a memory fading. Pay attention to any aspects that arise and treat them as separate dominoes, by tapping for each aspect separately. Make sure you tap on each event until it is resolved. If you find yourself unable to rate the intensity of a bad event on the 0-10 scale, you might be dissociating, or repressing a memory. One solution to this problem is to tap 10 rounds of EFT on every aspect of the event you are able to recall. You might then find the event emerging into

clearer focus but without the same high degree of emotional charge.

3. After you have removed the biggest dominoes, pick the next biggest, and work on down the line.

4. If you can, clear at least one of your specific events, preferably three, daily for 3 months. By taking only minutes per day, in 3 months you will have cleared 90 to 270 specific events. You will likely discover that your body feels better, that your threshold for getting upset is much lower, your relationships have improved, and many of your old issues have disappeared. If you revisit specific events you wrote down in your Personal Peace Procedure journal, you will likely discover that the former intensity has evaporated. Pay attention to improvements in your blood pressure, pulse, and respiratory capacity. EFT often produces subtle but measurable changes in your health, and you may miss them if you aren't looking for them.

5. After knocking down all your dominoes, you may feel so much better that you're tempted to alter the dosages of medications your doctor has prescribed. Never make any such changes without consulting with your physician. Your doctor is your partner in your healing journey. Tell your doctor that you're working on your emotional issues with EFT, since most health care professionals are acutely aware of the contribution that stress makes to disease.

The Personal Peace Procedure does not take the place of EFT training, nor does it take the place of assistance from a qualified EFT practitioner. It is an excellent supplement to EFT workshops and help from EFT practitioners. EFT's full range of resources is designed to work effectively together for the best healing results.

Is It Working Yet?

Sometimes EFT's benefits are blindingly obvious. In the introductory video on the home page of the EFT Universe website, you see a TV reporter with a lifelong fear of spiders receiving a tapping session. Afterward, in a dramatic turnaround, she's able to stroke a giant hairy tarantula spider she's holding in the palm of her hand.

Other times, EFT's effects are subtler and you have to pay close attention to spot them. A friend of mine who has had a lifelong fear of driving in high-speed traffic remarked to me recently that her old fear is completely gone. Over the past year, each time she felt anxious about driving, she pulled her car to the side of the road and tapped. It took many trips and much tapping, but subtle changes gradually took effect. Thanks to EFT she has emotional freedom and drives without fear. She also has another great benefit, in the form of a closer bond to her daughter and baby granddaughter. They live 2 hours' drive away and, previously, her dread of traffic kept her from visiting them. Now she's able to make the drive with joyful anticipation of playing with her granddaughter.

If you seem not to be making progress on a particular problem despite using EFT, look for other positive changes that might be happening in your life. Stress affects every system in the body, and once you relieve it with EFT, you might find improvements in unexpected areas. For instance, when stressed, the capillaries in your digestive system constrict, impeding digestion. Many people with digestive problems report improvement after EFT. Stress also redistributes biological resources away from your reproductive system. You'll find many stories on EFT Universe of people whose sex lives improved dramatically as a by-product of healing emotional issues. Stress affects your muscular and circulatory systems; many people report that muscular aches and pains disappear after EFT, and their blood circulation improves. Just as stress is pervasive, relaxation is pervasive, and when we release our emotional bonds with EFT, the relaxing effects are felt all over the body. So perhaps your sore knee has only improved slightly, but you're sleeping better, having fewer respiratory problems, and getting along better with your coworkers.

Saying the Right Words

A common misconception is that you have to say just the right words while tapping in order for EFT to be effective. The truth is that focusing on the problem is more important than the exact words you're using. It's the exposure to the troubling issue that directs healing energy to the right place; the words are just a guide.

Many practitioners write down tapping scripts with lists of affirmations you can use. These can be useful. However, your own words are usually able to capture the full intensity of your emotions in a way that is not possible using other people's words. The way you form language is associated with the configuration of the neural network in your brain. You want the neural pathways along which stress signals travel to be very active while you tap. Using your own words is more likely to awaken that neural pathway fully than using even the most eloquent words suggested by someone else. By all means use tapping scripts if they're available, to nudge you in the right direction. At the same time, utilize the power of prolonged exposure by focusing your mind completely on your own experience. Your mind and body have a healing wisdom that usually directs healing power toward the place where it is most urgently required

The Next Steps on Your EFT Journey

Now that you've entered the world of EFT, you'll find it to be a rich and supportive place. On the EFT Universe website, you'll find stories written by thousands of people, from all over the world, describing success with an enormous variety of problems. Locate success stories on your particular problem by using the site's drop-down menu, which lists issues alphabetically: Addictions, ADHD, Anxiety, Depression, and so on. Read these stories for insights on how to apply EFT to your particular case. They'll inspire you in your quest for full healing.

Our certified practitioners are a wonderful resource. They've gone through rigorous training in Clinical EFT and have honed their skills with many clients. Many of them work via telephone or videoconferencing, so if you don't find the perfect practitioner in your geographic area, you can still get expert help with remote sessions. While EFT is primarily a self-help tool and you can get great results alone, you'll find the insight that comes from an outside observer can often alert you to behavior patterns and solutions you can't find by yourself.

Take an EFT workshop. EFT Universe offers more than a hundred workshops each year, all over the world, and you're likely to find a Level 1 and 2 workshop close to you. You'll make friends, see expert demonstrations, and learn EFT systematically. Each workshop contains eight learning modules, and each module builds on the one before. Fifteen years' experience in training thousands of people in EFT has shown us exactly how people learn EFT competently and quickly, and provided the background knowledge to design these trainings. Read the many testimonials on the website to see how deeply transformational the EFT workshops are.

The EFT Universe newsletter is the medium that keeps the whole EFT world connected. Read the stories published there weekly to stay inspired and to learn about new uses for EFT. Write your own experiences and submit them to the newsletter. Post comments on the EFT Universe Facebook page, and comment in the blogs.

If you'd like to help others access the benefits you have gained from EFT, you might consider volunteering your services. There are dozens of ways to support EFT's growth and progress. You can join a tapping circle, or start one yourself. You can donate to EFT research and humanitarian efforts. You can offer tapping sessions to people who are suffering through one of EFT's humanitarian projects, like those that have reached thousands in Haiti, Rwanda, and elsewhere. You can let your friends know about EFT.

EFT has reached millions of people worldwide with its healing magic but is still in its infancy. By reading this book and practicing this work, you're joining a healing revolution that has the potential to radically reduce human suffering. Imagine if the benefits you've already experienced could be shared by every child, every sick person, every anxious or stressed person in the world. The trajectory of human history would be very different. I'm committed to helping create this shift however I can, and I invite you to join me and all the other people of goodwill in making this vision of a transformed future a reality.

EFT on a Page

1. **Where in your body** do you feel the emotional issue most strongly?

2. **Determine the distress level** in that place in your body on a scale of 0 to 10, where 10 is maximum intensity and 0 is no intensity:

10, 9, 8, 7, 6, 5, 4, 3, 2, 1, 0

3. **The Setup:** Repeat this statement 3 times, while continuously tapping the Karate Chop point on the side of the hand (large dot on hand diagram below):

   "Even though I have _____ (name the problem), I deeply and completely accept myself."

4. **The Tapping Sequence:** Tap about 7 times on each of the energy points in these 2 diagrams, while repeating a brief phrase that reminds you of the problem.

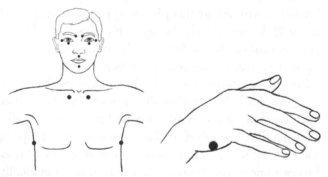

5. **Determine your distress level** again on a scale of 0 to 10 again. If it's still high, say:

   "Even though I have some remaining _____ (problem), I deeply and completely accept myself."

6. **Repeat from Step 1** till your distress level is as close to 0 as possible.

   Find dozens of tap-along videos at EFTUniverse.com

I would like to thank Dawson Church, PhD, for his gracious permission to use herein *The EFT Mini-Manual* from EFT Universe. For a free printable download of this manual, visit EFTUniverse.com. Along with the free download, you can sign up for the free *EFT Universe Insights Newsletter,* which contains numerous success stories from people using EFT. This information will inspire and instruct you in trying EFT on everything!

Modifying the EFT Setup Statement

In tapping with fellow Christians, I find that many of them object to the Setup phrase "I completely and deeply accept myself" (the affirmation part of the Setup Statement). At times, it is the deal-breaker as to whether a Christian will tap, as this phrase appears to deeply offend many Believers. Early in my EFT practice, this Setup phrase rankled me a bit too. As it simply did not feel right, I've since changed the Setup Statement to better reflect our understanding of who we are in Christ. When I experienced the "aha" realization of how best to adapt this protocol for fellow Christians, I believe this book was conceived in my mind at that moment. The Holy Spirit was talking to me and, to address this objectionable issue, I have some suggestions for Setup phrases specifically for use by Christians.

As I'll share with you here (and as you discovered in *The EFT Mini-Manual*), the affirmation or self-acceptance Setup phrase has a specific use: to remove psychological reversal. Psychological reversal tends to manifest when the person doesn't feel an appropriate emotional response in relation to what he/she is claiming to have experienced or be feeling, or the EFT healing process slows down or stops.

Here's an example. A client who was raped and has an understandable complaint of great emotional distress but is sitting in my office calmly, devoid of facial affect, with no emotion in her voice as she relates the story of the assault to me, is probably psychologically reversed. There is an emotional disconnect happening here. I would expect this client to be crying uncontrollably as she recalls the rape incident. The fact she isn't tells me there is some kind of emotional dissonance happening. It shows she has blocked off the event, locking it away in some part of her mind, hoping to keep the pain at a minimum, and away from her everyday functionality. It's a natural way the subconscious deals with our extreme pain. It simply disconnects certain memories from the frontal cortex of the brain so we are no longer aware of a traumatic event. This is an emotional survival instinct God implanted in us.

I encourage all new tappers to use the Setup Statement each time they tap. It helps you craft and clarify what the problem is and precisely what you are feeling about the problem. I recommend using a Christian acceptance phrase instead of the classic Clinical EFT one. Use one of my examples below or craft one of your own. There are no "magic" words here. It's the actual tapping that clears the emotions as you tune in to how you feel about the problem you are addressing.

Here are some Setup Statements of my own:

Even though I have this emotion (personalize this) *about this problem* (add in your own issue here), *I know God loves and accepts me; therefore, I accept (and love) myself.*

Even though I have this emotion (personalize this) *about this problem* (add in your own issue here), *I confess my sin and accept the forgiveness of the God of the Universe, my Savior and Redeemer, who calls me His beloved.*

Even though I have this emotion (personalize this) *about this problem* (add in your own issue here), *I know God loves me and accepts me just the way I am; therefore I accept myself and all of my emotions as God created me.*

Even though I have this emotion (personalize this) *about this problem* (add in your own issue here), *Jesus loves me and died for me on the Cross of Calvary; therefore I accept myself as God created me with all my emotions.*

The Setup Statement uses elements from other psychological processes such as exposure to the problem and a cognitive shift with the acceptance statement. As you create your own personalized Setup Statement, just be sure to include these two elements: exposure to the problem and some kind of acceptance statement. Doing so makes your subconscious aware of exactly what you want to deal with as you tap, and this also aids in your focus.

As you continue the EFT tapping, feel free to use Christian wording for the Reminder Phrases if that appeals to you, such as: *"I cover this fear with the redeeming blood of Jesus," "I cover this emotion with the work of the Cross," "I'm breathing in Your love and grace for this anxiety,"* or *"I breathe out this anxiety* (or other emotions) *and I breathe in Your love and mercy."* Personalize the statements by adding in a component that matches your faith. Just be sure you name the "emotion" you feel or the "event" you are tapping. My preference is to use the emotion itself; but either way, you are exposing yourself to how this problem affects you, employing proven Clinical EFT techniques to purge and release the emotions associated with the problem.

I suggest using a three-pronged approach: 1) tapping, 2) stating the negative, and 3) covering the issue with the blood of Jesus.

You will also begin to recognize when you need or don't need to use the Setup Statement. My personal use of it is limited now as, once mastered, I primarily utilize it in cases where a client feels little or no emotion in response to a problem for which one would normally have a significant emotional reaction (the psychological reversal previously referenced).

I also suggest you open and close your tapping sessions with prayer. I finish all the short prayers off with "In Jesus' name" just like we always pray. Here are a few abbreviated examples you might want to use or modify for your own tapping sessions:

1. "Heavenly Father, we ask your presence at our session today. Help us address anything that might hin-

der our walk in Your will. Guide us. Fill us with Your Spirit."

Closing prayer: "Father, God of the Universe, let your peace permeate this place, this person, this life, in Jesus' name."

2. "Gracious God and Creator, we ask you to move us in a healing pathway that you would have us follow. Open up a direct line to this healing today."

Closing prayer: "Father and God of Your children, let all things be done today to bring glory to Your name and to the work You would have us do in the world. Let nothing hinder this special task."

3. "Almighty Father, we ask your presence as we meet and tap and pray for Your guidance. All things are in Your hands and we ask Your help in the name of Jesus."

Closing prayer: "Our Lord and God, let your blessings and healing power now flow into _____'s life today and in the week ahead."

4. "Lord of all heaven and earth, we thank You for our wonderfully created bodies, and ask You now to help us as we tap for health and healing of body, soul, and spirit that we might live more victoriously in this world."

Closing prayer: "God of the Universe, let _____ now rest in Your care, and may you continue transforming _____ into your likeness."

5. "Glorious King, You reign over all things. We ask Your intervention now as we seek to bring into the

light and cleanse areas of concern as only Your touch can do. By the blood of Jesus, we pray."

Closing prayer: "Father God, let us linger in Your Spirit and power and strength. Let it direct every facet of _____'s life by the power of what Jesus did for us on the Cross."

6. "Heavenly Father of all, guide us and lead us. Let your presence be here among us, Your wisdom and strength filling every cell and fiber of our beings. In Jesus' name..."

Closing prayer: "May the same Father and God who is Creator and Keeper of the world bless you with His power, shine His face upon you, and grant you peace."

7. "God of your people and the Keeper of Your sheep, be with us now as we lift _____ to Your throne to help us during this time of tapping and prayer. Refresh, renew, and heal in Jesus' name and through the wonders of the bodies that you have given us."

Closing prayer: "Dear Jesus, now let _____ go out into the world around us. Cover _____ with Your grace."

8. "Almighty God and Father, all provision is in Your hands, that's why we call You Jehovah Jireh. Provide for us now in this time as only You can. And we offer our heartfelt thanksgiving."

Closing prayer: "King of the universe and our hearts, let us be of one mind with You and reflect this healing to others."

9. "Creator and Ruler of heaven and earth, You took great care in making us in Your image. Help us now as we seek to draw out emotions and feelings that might be a blockage for us as we walk in the path of your will. We revel in Your holy name."

Closing prayer: "Gracious God, give us peace at all times, make us able to draw from Your strength and walk in power along the path in this world, protected by Your angels and held close in Your loving hands."

General: "Heavenly Father, spread Your wings above me (us) and shield me (us) from any evil. Your mercy and love will not fail me (us). I (we) rest in Your almighty arms."

As you read and study the EFT instructions and examples in this book, remember to take personal responsibility for all aspects of your emotional and physical health. Use these techniques on smaller emotional problems first in order to familiarize yourself with the method and protocols.

The EFT Mini-Manual provides the basics of how EFT works, and you can get started straightaway with the one-page outline of tapping instructions ("EFT on a Page"). The techniques are fairly simple, but sometimes the issues needing to be addressed are more profound or complex in nature. In these instances, help from a professionally trained Clinical EFT Practitioner may be necessary to obtain thorough results. There is a database of certified Clinical EFT practitioners at EFTUniverse.com. In the future, I hope to compile a list of Christian EFT practitioners.

Incorporating Scripture into EFT

I know from my own firsthand experience as well as the experiences of my clients that we cannot spiritually repair any relationship with another human being until we fix the vertical relationship with our heavenly Father. Once tapping has neutralized the negative emotions, scriptural affirmations and protocol statements or verses work very well. After that comes the humility, exemplified by Jesus washing the feet of His disciples (John 13). Washing of the feet in Jesus' time was symbolic of spiritual cleansing and encompassed His humility in the washing act itself. EFT is an emotional cleansing that God uses to draw us closer to Him spiritually, but we must humble ourselves and ask for His help.

I want to make this perfectly clear. Once EFT has done its emotional work, I have found, and others have wholeheartedly agreed, God literally feels so much closer. God hasn't moved; you have! Once the emotional pain is pulled out of your life, you will find you have a huge capacity to now "feel" God. There is actually room for Him in your life. Lives stuffed full of emotional trash leave little space for a relationship with the God of the universe. Too often, we humans are so busy worrying our way from one project or activity to the next, one day to the next, or allowing an emotional response to be triggered by this person's statement or that person's action that God is the farthest thought from our minds.

When EFT does its work, all that old triggering baggage no longer holds you captive. You aren't stuck hauling around those emotionally weighty cement boots any longer. The heaviness is gone. God takes it away, leaving you free to prance, dance, and delight in Him like King David did. You feel God nearly constantly. It promises to be the most freeing experience of your life! I can tell you this because it happened to me—God delivered me! And He can do the same for you!

After all, we have this assurance, "As far as the east is from the west, so far has he removed our transgressions from us (Ps. 103:12), and He faithfully remembers them no more: "I, even I, am He who blots out your transgressions, for my own sake, and remembers your sins no more" (Isa. 43:25). If the Lord remembers them "no more," then why should we continue to carry around the emotional consequences of those sins, beating ourselves up day after day? Jesus told us in John 10:10(b), "I have come that they might have life and have it to the full." God can heal us spiritually and emotionally through EFT, if we avail ourselves of this wonderful gift.

Scriptures direct us to the source of the blessings, the cleansing of trouble spots in our lives, cleaning out the debris from our bodies, which are temples of the Holy Spirit ("Do you not know that your body is a temple of the Holy Spirit, who is in you, whom you have received from God," 1 Cor. 6:19), strengthening our physical and emotional attributes, extending kindness and compassion, and following the example of Jesus toward others—these are just some of the areas where Christian EFT can be effective.

Tapping verses from His word can be very helpful here. Nearly every night as I do my own personal devotions, I tap my way through them. The following are some examples of faith statements and Scripture verses that can be used while tapping.

Statements of Faith

Fill me with your Holy spirit and His love, joy, peace, and strength.

I surrender up myself to you so that You can live and work through me, Lord.

I dedicate my body, soul, and spirit to you.

I receive Your healing this moment.

I lift up my voice in praise to You for what You have done for me.

I thank You in advance for the blessings that You will pour upon my life (today).

I lift up and open my hands to receive Your might, Your miracles, and Your blessed healing.

Your kingdom come, Your will be done through me today.

May Your power and Your miracles be made manifest in my life this day.

I bow before You in thanks for the forgiveness You have washed over me.

With that forgiveness, I thank You for making me Your special vessel and Your temple here on earth, Lord.

Scriptural Statements

You are the Shepherd who provides all that I need. (Ps. 23:1)

You restore my soul and lead me in paths of righteousness. (Ps. 23:4)

I forgive those who have wronged me, as God forgives all of us. (John 20:23)

I am adopted as Your son/daughter through Jesus Christ. (Eph. 1:5)

Take heart, son, your sins are forgiven. (Matt. 9:2)

The Lord illumines my darkness. (2 Sam. 22:29)

The Lord quiets me by His love; He will rejoice over me with gladness. (Zeph. 3:17)

I have unity of mind, sympathy, brotherly love, a tender heart, and a humble mind. (1 Pet. 3:8)

I choose to live for Him (Jesus). (Rev. 4:1)

Jesus fills my life with all good things according to His purpose. (Eph. 5:18b)

I hope that the Setup and concluding statements as well as the scriptural and faith statements have given you an idea as to possible entrances and exits that can be used for an actual tapping session. As the transformative power of EFT is best illustrated by the real-world healing it delivers to people who've suffered from a wide range of complaints and issues, however, what follows is a collection of case histories from my client files. See if their struggles remind you of struggles of your own (or perhaps of someone you know). And get ready to be amazed!

5

Using EFT to Heal Emotional Traumas and Disturbing Memories

As you learned in the previous chapter, there are seven face and upper body tapping points. Humans use all seven when we find ourselves in emotional distress. We naturally gravitate to these points.

Let me give you several examples. When we get a migraine, we tend to put our fingertips (which are extra tapping points too) above our eyes to ease the pain and soothe us. We apply pressure to the eyebrow tapping point. When we receive bad news, we place our hands over our mouth and upper lip. Two tapping points are touched there: the chin point and the one under the nose. Other times when we feel exasperated, we place our hand over our forehead. Again, we have touched one, if not two of the tapping points. Every time we touch these points, we are self-soothing. That touch can be similar to the method of using acupressure.

When upset or anxious, some people wring their hands. On the upper edge of each fingernail are tapping points, so by the wringing action, we stimulate those tapping points, too. Chewing the fingernails also stimulates those acupressure points. Anxiety or fear tends to prompt many people to chew their nails or cuticles. When anxious or embarrassed, others place their hands over their entire face. In that position, nearly all the face tapping points have just been touched or rubbed, again administering self-soothing. There are other examples, but you now see the idea.

We engage in all these actions "instinctively," or so we've been taught. I believe they are instead universal self-control methods God instilled in us when He created the human race on the sixth day of Creation, but we still don't know or science hasn't yet discovered all the intricate workings that God in His wisdom designed in us when He formed man from clay.

The physiology involved in EFT (see Chapter 2) goes to the heart of how perfectly God created us! While we Christians may not want to use the Chinese/Eastern explanation of meridians, I believe we should understand and embrace the anatomical and physiological explanation of why and how EFT works, and in this way we can celebrate yet another aspect of God's creativity. He who spoke the universe into existence out of nothing created us, and I believe He designed EFT as a means of keeping us healthy and in harmony during our time here on earth.

As your subconscious controls 95% to 97% of your life without any conscious input from you (Lipton, 2008, p. 33), most of this is manifested in the autonomic mechanisms of simply remaining alive: heart beating, lungs breathing, muscles moving, blood circulating, food digesting. None of us think about these actions, nor do we control them. God took care of those intricately critical details in the design of our bodies! We'd wear ourselves out if we had to think about breathing or circulating our blood, wouldn't we?

The subconscious has another job it does for us, one that we don't think about either! It is in the business of protecting us, keeping us alive and away from danger. What that means is your subconscious decides what you need to know and when you need to know it. It is running your life! The subconscious buries everything it thinks is a threat to your survival or a threat to your emotional well-being. It simply will not allow you to think about the issue or event any longer, even if it is unconsciously causing you distress or controlling your life in some uncomfortable or habitually bad way. The subconscious doesn't care! It doesn't work to make your life comfortable in the way you think it should. Instead, its primary goal is simply to keep you breathing and functioning.

Now, enter emotionally negative events: childhood (or adult) verbal abuse, physical abuse, rape, sexual abuse, posttraumatic stress disorder (PTSD), a car accident, a loved one's death, or just about anything in life that was scary, horrifying, upsetting, or anxiety-producing. We all have this stuff. Your stuff is merely a variation of my stuff! The subconscious conveniently helps us "forget" these events ever happened, especially if they were overwhelming. Your conscious mind cannot deal with this level of anxiety, particularly if the situation causing the distress is repetitive in nature (e.g., prolonged abuse). The subconscious shuts your thinking mind down, blanking out the problems, and burying the accompanying emotions and memories. This response to a trauma doesn't make you mentally ill or mentally unstable; it makes you human!

Kathy's Story: Buried Memory of Teenage Trauma

Kathy's case illustrates how the subconscious makes us forget and also how the counterbalancing use of EFT makes us remember and then neutralizes that memory for our betterment.

At a recent professional conference, several of us, Kathy and I included, were enjoying a meal together. I knew none of the women at the table but, in my usual fashion, I opened conversation by asking what involvement within the community each participant had. Eventually, someone asked me what I do. I launched into my best EFT definition, one I've used multiple times.

All the gals listened politely, a couple asked a few short questions, and the meal ended. The following day I encountered Kathy again. She asked me what breakout session I was attending because she couldn't make up her mind. I told her what I had picked. Later in the day we ended up sitting next to each other at the same breakout session.

The session was over an hour in length, but somewhere in the middle of it I could see Kathy becoming more and more agitated. Obviously, the emotional issues being discussed were triggering something in her. She leaned over to me a couple of times, asking brief questions. I indicated to her that maybe I had something that would help. With her final lean-over, Kathy said, "We have to talk."

As we left the session, Kathy told me as we walked out the door, "I'm going to throw up." She mentioned this several times. I asked what had been triggered for her during the session. She had no idea except she wanted to vomit. It was suppertime, and I was hungry, so I asked her, "Do you want to eat, or do you want to tap?" I knew tapping was the best option for her, and Kathy chose wisely. We were going to tap.

We found a quiet spot to work. Now, remember, until about 8 hours before Kathy had never even heard of EFT, let alone tapped on an issue in her life. She was a professional counselor.

I gave her the quickest instructions I've ever done, and we commenced tapping. These included asking her to tell me anything that came to her mind no matter how offbeat, unclear, or disconnected it might seem, I wanted to hear what was going on in her subconscious. I asked what emotion she was feeling, but Kathy couldn't identify anything except, "I'm going to throw up."

I started with how her stomach felt. She gave me all kinds of descriptions of what it felt like. As an RN, I understand any graphic physical description, gross as they might be! She wriggled in her chair while we tapped a few minutes until the edge was off. I wasn't sure whether she wanted to bolt for the bushes or not, as we were sitting outside tapping.

I asked her to tap quietly for a few minutes and ask her subconscious what the stomach issue was all about: What did it want to tell her? Within 30 seconds, Kathy said she'd had two incidents at 4 years old, adding, "But I've resolved one of them."

"Okay, so which one do you want to work on?" I asked.

"Me being trapped in the woods with the teenage boys" was Kathy's answer.

Oh, great, I thought, I get a sexual assault right out of the box with this woman who knows absolutely nothing about EFT!

Before she started talking, she told me she wasn't sure whether "anything" had really happened in those woods because she could never remember that part. I asked her if she wanted to go there, as she might find out that answer. "Yes, let's do it" was her reply.

For not having any clue how EFT worked, Kathy was a champ. Without much prompting from me, she began giving descriptive details (aspects) of the incident. I did ask her to go back and find a neutral spot before it all started (EFT's Tell the Story Technique), which she did.

"Mom was on the phone crying, and I didn't know what was wrong," she told me. "Next thing I remember I'm in the woods with three 14-year-old boys trying to get me," she explained. The stomach nausea shifted to her upper chest, as the anxiety appeared to set in. "I can smell the train's diesel fuel and I can smell the pine trees."

I inquired what she was doing. "I'm crabbing backwards to get away from them. They are reaching for me," she said. Kathy was in obvious distress. I could see the story unfolding on her contorted face. So we just tapped for a few minutes to bring down her 10 SUD rating. To review, the SUD (subjective units of distress or discomfort) scale is 0 to 10, with 0 being no distress or discomfort, and 10 being the most distressing.

We then tapped for several minutes on the "crabbing backwards" part of the memory. Once again, I asked what details she was seeing and smelling. "The diesel and pine smell is gone," Kathy answered. I knew then that the issue was dissipating. "What do you feel under your hands?" I asked. "The pine needles are soft," came her reply. I asked her to describe the boys to me. "I can't see their faces, but they have brown hair, and are wearing long pants and short-sleeve shirts."

We kept tapping on the physical sensations she was experiencing. Still, Kathy could not tell me a single emotion around this incident. She was still wriggling and bouncing around in her chair, so I knew she was vividly picturing the incident in her mind.

There was no clock nearby, but probably within 15 minutes, Kathy's eyes popped wide open and she said with a great big smile, "I got away!" I questioned her to make sure she meant exactly what she said. "Yes, *nothing happened*. I got away!"

"How do you feel?" I asked.

"Great!" she replied. "I can't believe this! I've carried that around all my life and nothing even happened. I never knew. I've thought about this incident every single day of my life. That's solved!"

Immediately, she went to the second incident at 4 years old that she had said was "resolved," as it had snapped into focus for her.

"Do you want to tap on that one too or do you want to go eat dinner with everyone else?"

She opted to tap, so we started in on the next memory. I will sum this one up for you, but as you will see later, these memories were related.

When Kathy was a child, a toddler she didn't know was hit by a car near where she lived. Instead of using chalk to outline the body on the road, the police had used white paint. And that paint had staying power! Every day Kathy remembers asking her mom why the little boy didn't get up off the road. Being so young, like all children, she couldn't process information the way adults do. At 4 years of age, she was living in the theta and alpha brain wave state. Toddlers only suck in information; they don't put the pieces of incidents together. In Kathy's young mind, that little boy was literally lying on that street!

All Kathy's mom kept saying to her at the time was "Be careful." Whatever "be careful" means to a 4-year-old!

We tapped on the white paint outline, on her mother's words, and the pressure she felt in her chest. I finally got an intuitive hit, and said, "Where was his mommy?" Kathy jumped on that like a bee on honey.

We tapped for another 10 or so minutes on different aspects of this story, when, as with the first memory, Kathy's eyes widened and she said, "I'm okay, it's better, now let's go eat. I'm hungry. I know what this is. My grandmother lost a 12-year-old child and it's tainted our lives ever since." As a professional mental health worker, and to some of us medical people, when we are done with something, we are done. Kathy was now simply done with these memories!

The next morning I ran into her again. She greeted me with these words, which made me smile: "I thought of you when I woke up this morning and then I started to cry again. I went into the shower and tapped and cried. I know what all of this is about now. The pieces finally fit. Where was my mommy? Where was my mommy when those three 14-year-old boys had me cornered in the woods? I see it all now. Thank you so much. I'll be in contact. I have to get certified to use EFT with my clients. I have never seen anything like this. EFT's amazing!"

Kathy subsequently contacted me for EFT Universe certification information. Later, I spoke with her on the phone and she told me when she returned home she related her EFT experience to her oldest daughter. Turned out, her daughter knew all about EFT. A local therapist had used it on her daughter 3 or so years ago when dealing with an OCD (doctor-diagnosed obsessive-compulsive disorder) issue. "By the way, my daughter's OCD is gone now," Kathy added.

I was thrilled that another professional therapist could see the efficacy of EFT based on firsthand experience. She e-mailed me, saying, "I can't believe it. I recall those two memories now and I have no emotion about either one of them anymore. That session changed my life. It might not be a big deal for you, but it's a *huge* deal for me."

As you can see from this story, there is a problem in the forgetting! The subconscious remembers every single detail of every single thing you have ever done or that has happened to you. It is rerunning those memories as though they are current events. These memories can, and most likely are, influencing every hour of your present-day life, and it could well be to your detriment because those negative memories are impacting how you handle today's issues. As Christians, we want to and try to lay all of these ungodly emotions or events at the foot of the Cross, but, when caught in this cycle, our subconscious keeps going back and picking them up again and again.

"For I do not understand my own actions. For I do not do what I want, but I do the very thing I hate" (Rom. 7:15). "For the desires of the flesh are against the Spirit, and the desires of the Spirit are against the flesh, for these are opposed to each other, to keep you from doing the things you want to do" (Gal. 5:17).

Why do we do this? Because it is learned programming, it is comfortable, it is what we know. The subconscious doesn't really like change. It keeps you doing what it knows from the past, and the evil one is happy this happens, as it keeps us trapped within ourselves and our negative memories. He uses it to his best advantage whenever he has the opportunity to do so.

Now each and every time you encounter that trapped behavior or a similar one—years later—your subconscious reacts the exact same way it did when the behavior first happened. This is learned cognition. And, guess what? You will feel the same feelings you experienced at the time of the original event.

To review the discussion in Chapter 2, your body's neurochemistry mixes up a specific brew of neurotransmitters, hormones, and peptides—ligands (Pert, 1997, p. 23)—to match the feelings or emotions, such as fear, anxiety, grief, sadness, panic, disappointment, or abandonment. As you relive those same memories or events over and over again, your body reproduces that same ligand mix, causing you to build a vibrant negative neural pathway, making it easier and easier to pull up those specific emotions repetitively. Thus you repeat the same behavior and thought process. You are emotionally stuck in the same rut with no apparent way out.

As Christians, we try to change our thinking process, but when we can't, guilt sets in and we then blame ourselves for our lack of faith. The downward emotional spiral has begun. Satan is happy to have us this way and will contribute any negative thinking he can to worsen the problem. Tapping, mercifully, breaks this cycle.

Julia's Story: Incest Victim

A 48-year-old client called me for help. As Julia understood she was out of control and her life was quickly slipping in a direction she no longer wanted it to go, she drove over 90 minutes for this appointment. We had corresponded several times via e-mail about what EFT is and what it could do for her and even tapped once a year before for just a few minutes over an anger issue surrounding her mom. Due to schedules and geography, she couldn't pursue further appointments at that time. A year later, Julia was now willing to make the necessary effort to have an in-person session.

She arrived 45 minutes late to the appointment, but I had blocked out several hours for her, not knowing how long this tapping session would be or where it would lead us. I knew from previous conversations and e-mails she had numerous issues to address. We began tapping within minutes of her arrival and I opened the session with prayer as I always do when dealing with a Christian client.

Immediately, as I started her tapping on her collarbone, allowing her to talk a bit about her concerns, she launched into "My life is so confused. I'm stuck. Everything has stalled out including my career and my personal life. I realized I have a huge problem and I need help now. My GP wants me to go see a psychologist for cognitive behavioral therapy, but I want to try this first." I informed her that she was free to make the choice to see a psychologist and assured her I certainly would not stand in her way; in fact, I suggested she do so if she thought it might help her. She again stated she wanted to use EFT for now.

She indicated her family had "so many secrets" and no one was supportive of the other. Julia was sick and tired of the lack of transparency within this large family of hers. Everyone hid and pretended nothing was wrong, but many of her siblings had alcohol issues. Sadness was the emotion this evoked and it was a 9 on the SUD scale, along with a 7 for the feeling of confusion.

We tapped several rounds on "confusion" and "sadness" followed by a round of "remaining sadness and confusion."

Julia then dropped the bombshell that she felt "devastated because I have no memories of my childhood and I know it's directly related to the sexual molestation issue that occurred when I was 6 or 7. I don't remember much about it. I know something happened, but why didn't Mom stop it?"

Julia jumped to disliking her mother for not doing anything about this. "And why didn't the other boys see what was going on and stop it?" she asked. Her anger was easily a 10 and so we began tapping on that.

TH (top of the head): *Where was Mom?*

EB (eyebrow): *Why didn't she protect me?*

SE (side of the eye): *Did I mean so little to her?*

UE (under the eye): *Did I mean so little to her?*

UN (under the nose): *She didn't care. Where was she during all this?*

CH (chin crease): *I was so insignificant to Mom.*

CB (collarbone): *I was so insignificant to Mom.*

UA (under the Arm): *I obviously meant nothing to her. Was she completely blind?*

I had hit a raw nerve with the word "insignificant." Julie acknowledged that was her deepest thought. With the Holy Spirit's help, I had intuitively pulled it out of her. She sobbed and sobbed. I allowed her to cry until her tears slowed, and then she could say, "I'm so insignificant to Mom" without an emotional tone in her voice. Then we continued.

TH: *Where was Mom?*

EB: *Neither she nor Dad protected me.*

UE: *Where were my brothers?*

UN: *I'm so angry at all of them.*

CH: *Where was Dad? Working and drinking.*

CB: *I'm horribly anger.*

UA: *I'm f-ing angry at them all. I'd like to be mad at God, but I don't think I should.*

Lots of swear words can come out during a session, accompanying the anger and other emotions. I allow clients to say or do whatever they need to do to get to the core issue of their problem.

We did another two rounds using this same theme until her SUD score dropped to 0.

We tapped then on the devastation issue, which readily dropped from an 8 to a 2. At that point, I asked her what she was feeling. Not necessarily wanting to go right into the sexual molestation/incest issue so soon in the session, I hoped to get some of her other emotions out of the way for her first. Then we would tackle the molestation using a gentle, sneaking-up approach.

I was a tad surprised that she jumped right into the incest issue by saying, "I know this is at the heart of it. I can't go a day without this issue popping up. It won't go away."

Okay, it was out in the open now, so I asked Julia what emotion there was on the issue and did she want to tell me the details (the Tell the Story Technique) or would she prefer not to divulge them (the Movie Technique). Her emotion was emptiness or indifference and it was a 10 SUD rating.

She went on to tell me there weren't enough details to tap on the incident, as all she remembered was her mom sent her into her brothers' bedroom to wake up the boys, as she typically did every morning when she was age 6 or 7. This time, her brother Allen asked her if she ever saw a penis before and would she like to see his. Allen was 17. What happened after that she doesn't remember, but she was told, "It went on for a while, whatever that meant."

Julia sidestepped the issue a bit by continuing with her own gentle technique. "I learned early that sex is something I can use. I traded a kiss in second grade for gum and pop. I devalued myself and it makes me quite sad, meaning I have no self-esteem." It was her session, so I just let her go where she felt she needed to go.

Here was a lot of tapping fodder, so we immediately began tapping:

TH: *I traded a kiss for gum and pop.*

EB: *I prostituted myself in second grade.*

SE: *I had no self-esteem.*

UE: *I already figured out sex would get me somewhere.*

UN: *I prostituted myself early on.*

CH: *I'm so sad I did this to myself.*

CB: *I devalued myself.*

UA: *I devalued myself and it makes me so very sad.*

We continued with:

TH: *I feel nothing anymore.*

EB: *I'm indifferent to life in general.*

SE: *I feel so empty inside. Oh, Jesus, I feel so empty inside.*

UE: *I have no self-worth.*

UN: *I'm worthless.*

CH: *I'm so worthless, I'm a reject.*

CB: *I'll never be worth anything again because I've never been worth anything in the past.*

UA: *I'm completely worthless to myself and to everyone else.*

We stopped at that point to reevaluate, but I had Julia continue to tap while we talked. She indicated the statements that hit home. Going on with her story, she said, "I had no self-worth, and Allen started giving me drugs when I was 13. I was so promiscuous in junior high. I let the guys take advantage of me. Where was Mom then? She didn't see this happening right before her eyes?" Then she continued, "I left home 2 weeks before my 18th birthday, and by age 19, I was raped by my 60-year-old boss, that disgusting old man. What a pathetic life I've had! Allen and I have talked about this, with him denying much of his role, but I know the rape and molestation led indirectly to the abortion I had. It damaged my innocence permanently. Doesn't anyone see how keeping all these secrets just perpetuates the problems? I need to break this cycle for future generations, if only for my own kids' sake."

I wanted to tap a bit on that diatribe, but Julia launched right into the next subject, which was related in its own way. "Now my professional reputation is being called into question. I'm distracted and feel purposeless," she said. I asked if she felt vulnerable. "No, it's more a feeling of being inadequate."

"Failure?" I asked. She answered in the affirmative and then said, "There are two recent incidents that bother me greatly."

My reply is always that I will listen, but the client must continue to tap. Ranting works, if done correctly. Julia then related to me the two recent incidents, but I could well see how they were simply more of what she had told me about her childhood. It was that repetitively learned pattern.

We tapped:

TH: *That Mike incident was Dad with his finger in my face.*

EB: *You are a guest in my house.*

SE: *Alice told me how to write stuff and then she told me I was a disappointment.*

UE: *I'm a disappointment to everyone, me included.*

UN: *I value honesty and I will not brown-nose anyone.*

CH: *It felt like that parental authority thing.*

CB: *I was inadequate.*

UA: *I am inadequate and always will be.*

We tapped on "remaining inadequate," and then continued with:

TH: *I'm a failure.*

EB: *I failed my parents, my kids, and myself.*

SE: *I'm a big fat failure.*

UE: *I'm so distracted that I'm going to fail more.*

UN: *I'm repeating the family traits in my own workplace.*

CH: *I'm a failure. Does God see me as a failure, too?*

UA: *I'll never amount to anything in my life.*

We tapped on "remaining failure" and that 8 SUD issue dropped to 0.

I went back to the abortion Julia had in college, asking her what she felt about it. "I've worked all of that through with Mike. I know God has forgiven me. I know he was a baby boy, I just know. I don't feel I need to work on this much more," she told me. I then asked if she had any remaining emotion around the abortion, what would that emotion be? "That's easy, it would be remorse and regret. If I had to do it over, I would definitely have the baby," came her reply. "If you had any remorse and regret, what number between 0 and 10 would that be?" I asked. "Oh, definitely a 10," she answered quickly. "Then, Julia, we need to tap on remorse and regret! That issue is not gone." And we did just that.

This highlights one of the biggest issues I see with Christians and their emotions. We sincerely confess our sins to God and then assume God will always immediately take away the consequences of that sin; however, sometimes He does, and other times He does not. God works naturally as well as supernaturally. Why He does it one way for one of us, and another way for others, I have no explanation. God is God and He is free to dispense His loving grace in any manner He chooses to whomever He chooses. There is always a reason God does what He does.

I tell people to double test their emotions to make sure EFT really did completely heal the troublesome event. When experiencing any kind of remaining physiological response to a "healed" memory or incident, please tap on it. That way, you'll be certain the healing is fully complete before moving on.

TH: *Remorse and regret.*

EB: *All this remorse and regret over what I did.*

SE: *Remorse and regret.*

UE: *I killed that baby. Jesus, I'm so sorry I did that.*

UN: *It was my fault because it was my choice.*

CH: *I killed him. He was God's precious child.*

CB: *Remorse and regret.*

UA: *All this remorse and regret.*

We tapped a couple rounds on this theme, and then I did a round or two on "remaining remorse and regret." Julia's eyes softened a bit and I checked in to see what was happening. The remorse and regret dropped, but up popped a 7 on guilt. "I didn't like who I was back then," she said.

We tapped a few rounds on guilt, then sadness emerged again. We tapped again on sadness around the abortion, with a round or two of "remaining sadness and guilt."

In some ways, it appeared this session was jumping all over the board, but I could plainly see what Julia was doing. Her first symptom was "confusion." She was engaged in a total life evaluation here with me. Julia began as early as she could remember and went straight through to the present day. We tapped on every single emotion that reared its ugly head.

Once the sadness and regret subsided to nothing, Julia immediately brought forth "devaluation." This seemed logical to me after having just tapped on guilt associated with not liking who she was in college. "I'm repeating my behavior by medicating myself. I spend $10 a day on wine. I tell myself I have to stop, but I can't. Then I tell myself it's only $10 a day and I deserve it, even though we can't afford $200 to $300 a month on wine for me to fall asleep at 9:00 p.m. I also don't like myself or my housekeeping." We tapped on the devaluation of herself with phrases like "I don't like myself much," "I'm repeating my old behavior," and "I feel worthless."

Once again, Julia launched into another piece of her story, with me insisting she continue to tap while she explained all this to me. "My daughter confronted me the other night, asking why I just finished an entire bottle of wine myself. I couldn't answer her. I was stunned by the question. 'Why can't you stop drinking?' she asked me."

"It sounds like self-sabotage to me, do you agree?" I asked. She agreed wholeheartedly. I took a couple of minutes to explain to her how self-sabotage works and ended the explanation by telling her how EFT can break these self-destructive habits.

Julia identified "stupidity" and "insanity" as how she viewed her drinking. "Are those emotions?" she asked. I knew that some might not think so, but they were good enough for me, so we tapped on "I feel insane," "I've lost control," and "I'm so stupid for drinking so much."

Anger popped up next with her statement, "We create our kids' future. My kids are watching what I'm doing. I know better than this. I promised my daughter I would quit drinking and it's been 7 days today, but my daughter told me she doesn't know if it will last. I was sober for 12 years, and have been drinking again now for 6 years. God designed me for better than this. I need to submit to God and separate from my past. I want this to be the first day of my new life!"

This could indeed prove to be the first day of the rest of her life. It was no joke! EFT can and will break these emotional habits and I intended to help Julia do just that. We tapped through the SUD level of 8 for anger and frustration with overcoming obstacles and bad habits.

We had covered a lot of territory in these couple of hours. Because this is a Christian client, I ended the session with a good round of self-forgiveness. I had already asked her if she had confessed all these sins to God. She said she had, but still the guilt and pain had lingered before tapping. Hopefully, God has used EFT to neutralize all of those remaining leftover feelings of hers forever.

TH: *I know God has forgiven all my sins.*

EB: *He has cast those sins as far as the east is from the west as Psalm 103 says.*

SE: *I simply need to forgive myself. I'm way too hard on myself.*

UE: *I was just a kid. What did I know?*

UN: *A lot of this wasn't even my fault or my doing!*

CH: *No one protected me. I did the best I could with what I knew.*

CB: *God forgives me for the stuff that was my choice.*

UA: *I made bad choices.*

We continued:

TH: *I choose to make better choices now, ones that are in line with what God wants from me.*

EB: *God designed me for better than this.*

SE: *I submit to His ways now.*

UE: *He has forgiven me; I forgive myself.*

UN: *I am forgiven by God.*

CH: *I am forgiven by myself.*

CB: *I'm forgiven.*

UA: *I'm a forgiven sinner who is a redeemed saint.*

I did another round of "remaining forgiveness" and we ended the session, scheduling another for a week later. Julia reported feeling a peace like she had not felt for a very long time. She hoped it would last. I told her to let this session process in her mind and we would talk more the following week.

This protracted breakthrough session had lasted nearly 3 hours, much longer than I would normally do with any client—it was probably a record of some sort. But, after all, she had driven 3 hours round trip for this session!

We had covered a lot of emotionally charged territory, processing the following emotions: confusion, sadness, emptiness, indifference, lack of self-esteem, distraction, purposelessness, failure, vulnerability, inadequacy, remorse, regret, guilt, self-sabotage, anger, stupidity/insanity, insignificance, devaluation, and hatred. Nineteen to 20 different emotions of sorts were tapped on in one session!

As you read this case study, I hope you saw the correlation between the behavior/sin and the consequences of that sin. Allen did something God surely didn't want him to. That one action started a cascade of downhill, negative emotions and behaviors for his younger sister. Was that his intent? I doubt it. He was just a child himself at the time, but he nevertheless set Julia up for a lifetime of self-doubt, self-incrimination, and her own avalanche of bad choices stemming from this early sexual trauma.

This is where this God-given tool of EFT can help correct and reorient the Christian back onto the path toward Him. Many of us, including Julia, have tried many hours of "talk therapy" in a counselor's office. Sometimes all that "talking" retraumatizes us, ingraining the memory ever deeper, possibly doing more actual harm than good in the end.

Millie's Story: Childhood Issues with Mom

A friend phoned me in an excited state to talk about an EFT experience she'd just had. Millie had been working on her "stuff" for a couple years, moving along many childhood memories that had obviously impacted her life. Now, for the first time in her 50 years, she felt contented and reported enjoying freedom she'd never known before.

Apparently, Millie had been visiting at another friend's home, chatting away and allowing the time to get away from her. By the time she walked out of the house to her car, she realized over 2 and a half hours had passed, much longer than she had planned to stay for tea.

Suddenly, as she drove away, Millie realized a huge gush of guilt had flooded her. For once in her life, she took notice of it, making a mental note that she had to tap on this guilt when she arrived home.

This mental note is a signal to the subconscious that you heard its cry and you have every intention of listening to it in detail, allowing it to talk and inform you of exactly what else it wants released. The trick here is to follow through with what the subconscious considers a promise. Personally, I have found that if I don't honor that "promise," my subconscious always comes back with a bigger and louder complaint. It really does want to be heard!

Millie did indeed tap when she returned home after spending another hour shopping. She began by simply tapping on "all this guilt." The SUD level for the guilt wasn't particularly high, but a 4 is certainly enough of an issue to tap on. My practitioner rule is any issue that has a SUD score of 2 or higher should be tapped to make sure there are no other aspects or events underpinning the issue.

At my instruction, Millie took this opportunity to tap on her eyebrow point, asking herself what the source of this guilt was, assuming it was a childhood issue. Almost immediately, feelings of not being heard as a child popped up. No one ever had time to listen to anything she said or, at least, that was her adult perspective on it.

In her mind's eye, she saw the friend whose house she had just visited looking at the living room clock several times about halfway through the visit. Millie now asked herself, "Why didn't I take that as a hint I was sticking around too long?" Apparently, she hadn't, but that picture came to her mind, along with her friend's rather bland expressionless face.

Once that picture surfaced, the next scene was remembering her mother's own bland, expressionless face as Millie sat at the kitchen table doing homework as a child while her mom prepared dinner. Mom never appeared interested in anything Millie told her about school or about her friends. So disinterested was her mother that Millie doesn't remember her mother commenting one single time about any of it. This consistent lack of responsiveness left Millie with a sense of worthlessness and guilt. She felt so unimportant to everyone around her. No one wanted to listen to a thing she had to say.

Millie was now excited! This revelation gave her an opportunity to clear out another piece of the "I'm worthless" core issue she had carried around for decades. Another piece of that internal puzzle had just surfaced. It was all making more and more sense.

As simple as this case may sound to you, the reader, it is an important lesson in demonstrating how the sub-conscious will bring to you, almost on a big silver plat-ter, issues and feelings that contribute to how we see ourselves today, based on our experiences of yesterday. Mindfulness is the key here. Pay attention to those bumps, jiggles, spasms, twinges, and an occasion oddball pain that shoots through you throughout the day. Much of the time, it is your body telling you it has buried some-thing, probably a memory, in that body part. The body part is no doubt tired of hauling it around for you, and is simply asking you to relieve it of its burden. In learning to be mindful in this new way, you'll connect with your body and help it share its hidden issues with you as a result of your careful listening.

Take the few minutes necessary to be curious as to why that shooting pain went through your arm, leg, or belly. Ultimately, these practices may save you more grief than you can imagine. Take responsibility for your health, however. If you feel something physical may be posing a serious problem, it more than likely is, and you should seek medical help. Be aware of what your body is telling you. EFT is not a substitute for a medical doctor!

Carol's Story: Smell Triggers Negative Memories

Memories from past issues can be triggered by a scent. Here is another case from my files that illustrates how childhood memories are stored away, only to be triggered decades later in adulthood by sensory experiences. This doesn't happen consciously. Instead, these triggers occur beneath the cognitive awareness of the thinking mind.

My friend, Carol, related this story to me on the phone and I asked her to please type it up. It's a great illustration of how sensory input—in this case, a smell—can trigger either a positive or negative memory. Freshly baked cookies might remind us of our grandmother in her warm kitchen on the farm, or, as in this case, baked cookies that were frozen and thawed evoked a negative memory for Carol. She was then able to tap on it to clear another event in her life that wasn't quite so memorable.

Fact: The sense of smell (via olfactory nerves) is the only one of the senses with a direct connection to the amygdala, or alarm center, of the brain. All the other senses take about 15 processes to reach the amygdala, although that still happens in fractions of nanoseconds!

The following is Carol's story in her own words.

❊ ❊ ❊

Let me set the stage by relating an incident that happened to my uncle many years ago. He had spent a great deal of time lovingly training a parakeet he named Churkie for the sound that he made. Churkie could talk, whistle, speak German, do tricks, and walk from his owner's left hand up around the back of his neck and down to the right hand (called "walking the pike"), among other antics. This bird was indeed special and had taken a very long time to train, not to mention the patience needed.

Then one day it happened. Churkie was permitted to fly out of his cage and around the kitchen and was frequently given that opportunity. He was out and about one day as my aunt was cooking. She was making a huge kettle of soup, which was bubbling and steaming away. You can just about guess what occurred. Churkie was doing a low dive over to my aunt, crossing the kettle, and was apparently overcome by the steam, and fell into the pot. That horrific occurrence was never spoken of again.

I too had a parakeet and mine was named Timmy. I had been trying to train him, even though I was only 8 years old and I definitely did not have the patience for that kind of thing at the time. My track record with critters was not the greatest, but this one had survived the longest.

On a Saturday morning, my mother and I were going to walk to the streetcar stop to go downtown and do some shopping. This dates me just a little bit, doesn't it? But it was a common thing to do, just like heading downtown on a Friday night to buy groceries. It was my job to be sure that the little supper ham roast on the stove was turned off. As we walked to the corner and caught the bus, I thought I had turned it off. It was many hours before we returned home. On walking into the yard on the return trip, we could see fog through the windows—yellow fog. The small roast had cooked completely dry, and continued to over bake until smoke had poured throughout the entire house. The fire department was called, but thankfully no fire had begun, nor was my aged grandmother there at that time. However, Timmy was a fatality, having been overcome by the putrid smoke.

Now, the smoke smell is the basis of this story. It had permeated the house, leaving a yellow scum on things like the bathtub where a towel lying on the porcelain showed the white tub beneath it. Our clothes held a horrible smoky smell. The smell also lasted far too long. I felt terribly guilty that I had not double-checked the stove, causing all these smoke problems—but worst of all, I had caused the suffocation of my precious little bird. If I remember correctly, it was the last pet I ever had.

Tonight, years later, I was bringing cookies out of the freezer for a fundraiser. I had found a new cookie flavor, Cotton Candy, which sounded appealing for kids. In baking these, the house had acquired a nasty smell that, to me, smelled more like burnt cotton candy. As I thawed the cookies, I thought to check them. Opening up the bag nearly overcame me! There was a truly odd smell emanating from those cookies. Oh, yuck! I asked my husband to taste a piece. Maybe the frosting was spoiled? Dan said they were terrible. I tried a bite too and I totally agreed with him. I tossed out the cookies, and baked a new batch.

In the meantime, my stomach got horribly nauseated. When the new batch was finished baking, I sat down and thought, "What *is* that smell? Why is it nauseating me? This certainly is not the flu."

Sherrie had given me a good idea: Try to tap and find out the reason for the nausea. So I sat down on my rocking chair and did just that. I finally remembered the "smell" with my tapping. That very same dry, burned, choking smell from the ham roast on that fateful Saturday morning matched the awful smell in those Cotton Candy cookies. I tapped on guilt. I tapped on being responsible for all the mess. I tapped on my poor bird that died just like my uncle's in a tragic accident. I tapped on the nausea. I tapped on "my smoke-related headache." *"I totally and completely accept myself and forgive myself for being so careless and stupid."* I realized how grateful I was for the clear air I was now breathing and that there had been no fire on that day long ago, nor had any people been injured because of my negligence.

How interesting that a smell buried in my brain for decades could come to the surface after such a long time—it has to be over 50 years now! Just like a tangerine smell always reminds me of Christmas and the "goodie bag" after the church Christmas program. I also now remember the diesel smell of the long bus ride to and from school, the outside smell of laundry hanging on the clothes line that no fabric softener can match, the smell of the cigar my father smoked to relax on Sunday afternoons, and the musty smell of my grandma's bedroom. Each could well be another story, maybe even something to tap.

But tonight it was the cookies. Thanks to EFT, the nausea went away quickly and so did the headache. I was able to tap away the guilt and "loss" that my body mind had stored for all this time. Never would I have dreamed I would recall that incident in such detail. Until I learned EFT, I would have thought the memory was long since gone.

Thank You, Jesus, for forgiving me even though I haven't been able to ask until today. I can even recall the bird episode now without all that guilt. Thanks to my EFT practitioner, coach, and friend who told me what to do when I run up against something like this. I stand amazed at how God made us so intricately!

* * *

Paula's Story: Witnessed Dad's Tragic Death

As a member of a Christian medical organization (Lutheran Missions Attic Workshop), I was asked to give a speech about exactly what our group does. I agreed. The only business cards I had with me were my ones for EFT for Christians, so I tossed them, literally, on the tables for the ladies to take if they so desired.

I did my presentation as requested. As we finished with the follow-up questions, someone asked me, "What is this?" pointing to my business card. I asked if it was permissible for me to describe it. The group agreed for me to go ahead.

During the talk, an elderly lady began to cry. I, of course, noticed her, and inquired what was wrong.

Paula looked me in the eye, and asked, "You mean to tell me if we tapped, I can move some of these emotions I have about seeing my Dad killed before my very eyes when I was 7 years old?"

I grinned and told her, "Yes, I think I can help you. When do you want to tap?"

"Right now!" came her answer.

I was agreeable to tap immediately, as it was nearing dinnertime and the rest of the group was ready to go home. A few asked if they could stay to "watch." I gently told them I didn't think that would be a good idea and explained Paula and I needed to do this tapping privately.

We found a quiet corner in the building, and I went looking for some tissues plus a pen and paper, as I customarily take notes when conducting a session. I use these to go back to test and retest tapping results. I also believe I get a more thorough clearing sometimes because I more fully get into the client's story; this tool helps me later remember the six, eight, or ten different things we covered. I should add that I've never had a client ask me not to take notes. As a practitioner, note-taking is a personal choice, however.

With my usual MO, I opened with prayer and I asked Paula to begin tapping immediately. Some coaches dislike this because they feel it brings the emotions down too much, making it more difficult for the client to access what is going on in her memory. I personally find it achieves just the opposite. The tapping awakens the subconscious and alerts it to the fact help has arrived: It is time to tap, to remember, and to clear out emotional memories.

With that little crying question Paula originally asked, I didn't anticipate this to be a dry, tearless session. Her father's death? No way was this story going to be told without that box of Kleenex handy.

I inquired as to how old she had been when her father died. Paula answered, "I was 7, I saw it happen, and it has influenced my whole life since. There isn't a day that goes by that I don't think about that accident. And I know it negatively impacts my relationship with my husband and my children. I hover over them, fearful something bad will happen to them. I can't ever lose someone like that again. I know I have to leave things in God's hands, but I simply can't. Instead, I worry constantly."

"Paula, in your own words, please tell me what happened to your father. When you reach a part in the story that is really emotional for you, stop and we will tap until you are comfortable going on," I instructed her.

She began the story, "My dad was the most godly man I knew. He read the Bible to me, took us all to church, and treated us all so well. I adored him. He decided one weekend to help a neighbor man move to a new apartment. He took all of us kids along in order to give Mother a break. We loved being with Dad. Everything was loaded in the truck and I asked him if I could sit in his lap. He and my older brother were sitting on the open tailgate of the truck. Dad told me no and put me in the truck bed closest to the front cab.

"Off we started with the neighbor man driving. Suddenly, the truck hit a pothole. I heard the tailgate slam up and down, and then I saw both my brother and dad slide off the bouncing tailgate. My brother rolled, but dad went straight down on his back, hitting his head on the pavement."

As you can imagine, the tears began in earnest. I assisted Paula in tapping every single detail of those two paragraphs, until she could say them without any emotion in her voice.

She continued, "Finally, the man stopped the truck. Someone closed up the tailgate, trapping me in the truck. I hollered for them to let me out. Another man picked me up and set me down on the road. I saw Dad. He was lying still, with his head in a big puddle of blood."

Her crying understandably resumed at this point. Once again, I helped her tap down all the emotions around this part of the story. She grew calmer, blew her nose, and said, "Let's keep going." What a brave woman!

"A lady from across the street came to get me while all the commotion of the ambulance was happening. I don't know who called my mother. The lady sat me down on her porch steps and gave me some root beer and a cookie."

To break the tension a bit, I stopped her and said, "I bet you don't like root beer to this day, do you?" Paula looked at me, asking in an incredulous tone, "How did you know that?" I smiled and said, "Because root beer has been associated with this horribly negative memory, I knew you'd never drink it again." Paula looked at me like she had never thought of that before (and she probably hadn't). I then asked her to continue with the tale.

"The ambulance took dad away and I never saw him alive again. I know he was alive in the street because I could hear him moaning." Once again, her crying began, wrenching heartfelt sobs, her shoulders shaking, as if she were experiencing the incident right now in the present moment. Frankly, to her subconscious, she was—because, until this incident had EFT applied to it, her subconscious replayed this accident in her mind and in her body as if it were still occurring in the present tense, mercilessly, over and over again.

We repeated the tapping process, covering all the specific details of this particular part of the story until she settled down and her crying stopped.

At that point, she told me more about what happened to her family after her dad died, and how hard it was on her older siblings and her mom to keep food on the table. Paula's job was to watch the younger kids while everyone else went to work.

We continued to tap as she related the rest of the story details to me, but she never cried again. The "punch" had been pulled out of the incident.

I have no idea how long we tapped, but my best guess is about 40 minutes. I asked her one more time to tell me the whole story again, starting from a neutral place before her father loaded them all in the truck to help the neighbor.

Paula did as I instructed. Even she was surprised at how little emotion she had about the event at this point.

She stopped twice and commented about how different she now felt. I noticed that her emphasis on particular adjectives had lessened. In the retelling, she changed a few words that had a harsh meaning to something more subdued. "Terrible" was changed to "bad." "Huge puddle of blood" under her dad's head became just a "puddle of blood." We EFT practitioners see this quite often. Words change or soften once the emotion is pulled out of the traumatic event.

In the retelling of the story, Paula told me how mean this neighbor man had become after that accident, saying, "Why couldn't it have been him that was killed and not my dad? He began to drink a lot after that accident."

I asked her if she hated this man. In typical Christian fashion, Paula said, "Oh, no, we aren't allowed to hate." I asked again, "Do you hate this man? Tap and ask God if you do."

She complied, and then looked at me with wide eyes, saying, "You know, I *do* hate him. I never realized that!"

My Christian EFT process stepped in and I asked if she would like to confess that sin of hatred right here, right now, before God, and complete the process. Paula readily agreed!

I led her through a prayer of confession, in a simple manner, as God doesn't require lofty words. He just wants to hear us say from a sincere heart that we are genuinely sorry, and He will indeed forgive us. He always does! He's our heavenly Father.

I no more than finished the prayer when Paula said, "I never thought of this! No wonder that man was so mean and drank so much. He had a reason to do so." I replied, "Yes, because he felt responsible for your father's death."

Never have I seen such a beautiful grin as the one that spread across Paula's face at that moment. I knew in my heart God had just performed another of his miraculous healings through the power of His created EFT. My heart was bursting, knowing what I had just witnessed—the freeing of a sister in Christ from a haunting, lifelong event. Note that EFT's healing power is typically permanent if we do our work well.

Paula then explained to me in detail how this early childhood event had run her life. She told me all the fear and worry wrapped up in the accident had shaped her relationship with her entire family. She said she nagged her husband constantly. She knew in her heart she feared losing him, like she did her father, but she had not been able to stop the behavior. I suspected guilt had manifested in other areas of her life as well, even though we didn't tap on that emotion. Paula also told me she worries constantly about her adult children. She phones them frequently to check on them. Knowing they are in God's hands doesn't seem to calm her, causing her to feel like an inferior Christian as a result. This is where EFT can deliver such blessed relief.

A week later, I received a handwritten thank-you from Paula and I share it with you here:

> My burden has been lifted since our session together. I no longer feel like my witnessing of my father's accident is still happening over and over. I have been set free and know it happened,

but I don't relive it any longer. As for my feelings toward the neighbor man, hate is gone and so is the blame. I know all was in God's mysterious plan.

I live in the now and know I'm part of God's plan and He leads me. I tap and unload all other things that come up daily. We are so wonderfully made.

Thank you so much for helping me to help myself.

God bless you and all you do for others, Paula

Paula summed up in one small note nearly everything we teach about EFT's astounding results. It pulls the emotion out of our pasts, putting us in the here and now, living in the present, enjoying all that God gives us. Forgiveness and empathy tend to follow in the footsteps of tapping, giving us the ability to emulate our Savior when He went to the Cross on Calvary and carried all our sins there, securing our forgiveness.

Philippians 4:6 says, "Dismiss all anxiety from your minds. Present your needs to God in every form of prayer and in petitions full of gratitude." All our fears, anxieties, and worry are to be placed into His loving arms. It is His to carry. EFT gives us a God-given way to do just this, as Paula experienced in her tapping session.

Just as EFT released Paula of her lifetime of tormented memories, EFT has proven equally effective in treating children and can also be utilized to release kids from negative habits in order to keep these from being carried into their adulthood, as Amie's story illustrates.

Amie's Story: Scared to Sleep in Her Own Bed

Amie's mom and I met a year or so ago when I needed a substitute massage therapist. At that appointment, she told me about her 10-year-old daughter who had slept in bed with her and her husband for years. Amie would start out in her own bed each night, but within an hour or so come into her parents' bedroom and crawl into bed with them. Her mom had tried every technique, trick, and bribe she could think up to motivate Amie to stay in her own bedroom, without success.

Now that Amie was 10, a bigger issue had arisen. Friends wanted her to sleep over, but Amie had yet to spend an entire night outside her home, calling her mom to come get her and interrupting the sleep of all the adults involved. Worse yet, teasing over the issue had begun at school with all the accompanying embarrassment that entails for a child. Amie's mom called me to see what EFT could do about this persistent issue.

Given her age, getting Amie to talk at all was a challenge. Of course, she saw little reason to change her sleeping habits. I explained to her where to tap, why to tap, and asked her if she really wanted to get over this. I was hoping to get her to buy in to the process so she would tune in more completely. She indicated what she really wanted was to be able to do sleepovers with her friends. We thus arrived at our starting point in terms of her motivation.

Amie was mature enough to understand the SUD level, thus she indicated the level on not being able to do sleepovers was a 5 on the scale of 0 to 10. Sometimes when tapping with children, we use "spread hands" or drawings of "sad faces" to help them determine their SUD levels.

I had Amie begin tapping on the middle of her chest while we continued to talk. I was hoping to find an underlying issue that was contributing to this inability to sleep in her bed. I asked everything I could think of. Initially, I had Amie describe her bedroom arrangement. Did the closet bother her? Did a noise bother her? Was there something under the bed that was worrisome? On and on I went, trying to ferret out of my own childhood "freak-out" memories to assist me in my questioning. Had someone told her a scary story? Did a horror movie upset her? Finally, after about 10 minutes, I hit something—I brought up nightmares. Having danced around in her chair bored half to death until this point, Amie immediately perked up, looked me in the eye, and said, "Yes, when I was 3, someone touched me on the shoulder." And out it then came, "And I haven't slept in my own bed since then." Wow! I had uncovered the key issue! I asked more questions to get to the heart of the details so I could tap meaningfully for her.

Amie had a scared look in her eyes, so I inquired what her SUD level was for the "someone touched me" memory. She reported an 8. I allowed her to tell me the whole scary story. After she did, we tapped on the exact words she used.

Setup:

Even though something touched me on my shoulder when I was 3 years old and it freaked me out, I know Mom loves me.

Even though I think it was a person and there was no one else in the room but me, I jumped. I thought it was Dad goofing around with me, but he wasn't there, and I was scared. I know Mom loves me.

Even though I was scared half to death by whatever it was that touched me, I know it was there, because I felt it. No one is talking me out of this. I know Mom loves me.

TH: *I'm freaked out.*

EB: *Someone touched me on the shoulder.*

SE: *No one was there but me and my doll.*

UE: *I was so scared. Who could that have been?*

UN: *I was freaked out and I'm still freaked out when I think about it.*

CH: *I feel safe in Mom and Dad's bed. I don't want to be alone.*

CB: *Maybe that something will touch me again.*

UA: *I can't even go upstairs alone. Someone has to go with me.*

Amie took over telling me, "Maybe my dolly touched me. I haven't gone upstairs alone since I was 3. I'm freaked out. Someone touched my shoulder. No one was there, but someone touched me."

Then Amie began a bit of a reframe on her own. "Maybe it was my guardian angel that touched me. I believe in them, you know." We tapped a few times on the benefit of her guardian angel. Amie mentioned that being alone bothered her, particularly at night. We continued tapping on the "scared and nervous" part of her memory.

Amie's SUD level dropped to "0.5." As children will do, she abruptly indicated she was done with the session. She was hungry and wanted to go home now.

A week later, I contacted Amie's mom who told me, "The situation's better, but I think we need more work." Apparently, Amie started out in her own bed each night, but would still come into her parents' room, wanting to crawl into bed with them. Her dad would then take her back to her room. If he stayed until she fell asleep, she would finish the night in her own bed. In her mom's opinion, this was a significant improvement.

At the next appointment a week later, I learned that Amie was now sleeping in her own bed through the night!

Ten weeks after clearing the scary memory, I received an e-mail from Amie's mom telling me "all is well" with Amie, as she was now sleeping in her own bed with the only disturbance being her cat waking her up on occasion.

In most cases involving children, there is no need to do "formal" tapping like I did with Amie. Children clear quickly with EFT if we simply tap with them while they tell their story. There is no need to do a formal Setup. What works best is just tapping while they talk about whatever is bothering them, in their own words, at their own pace.

Tapping during bedtime prayer is another wonderful use of EFT. Allow your children to recount their day to you while you tap with them. Incorporate this practice into their nightly routine—read a devotion to them, pray with them, and then tap through their day with them.

If you have several children, have all of them tap together while one of them talks. All of you tapping will get what is called "borrowed benefits." We humans were created with something called "mirror neurons," which are nerve cells that cause people in a room to imitate each other, like when one person yawns, everyone else around the room yawns. As the one child relates his day and clears his emotions around an event, so the rest of the group clears their daily events as they tap along too. What a parental time saver!

By tapping regularly, not only do the children then not carry negative emotional burdens into adulthood, but they also learn a healthful habit—listening to one another in a caring manner!

The science behind Emotional Freedom Techniques teaches us how those early childhood experiences hold us fast, creating our adult reality without us understanding what makes us tick. The subconscious grabs an idea and stays with it throughout our lives until we realize life isn't giving us what we want or hoped to accomplish. For those of us who use EFT, we now know we can dismantle those early cognitive beliefs, changing everything and equipping us to lead an abundant, joy-filled life.

Young males are often the most difficult to tap with because they tend not to understand their emotions or what they are feeling, and often can't express them either. I worked with Andrew, a high school junior, for a few sessions around his blatant tardiness and poor grades. He chose not to continue tapping because the sessions just looked funny to him, but I found out from his mom that his GPA shot up to a 3.8 the next semester. It turned out to be temporary, but might it have stayed that high if we had continued tapping? It would have been great to find that out, as EFT works very well on performance issues. When I did tap with him, Andrew said little, except to relate to me about two dozen bullying events when he'd felt very picked on as a little child, so I simply reminded him to keep tuning into how he felt internally about those events.

Rather than working on the issue itself, EFT works on the emotions or feelings around the issue, as that is where the neural pathways change. As this newly discovered science continues to evolve with more and more research, I cannot wait to see all the healing miracles God is going to bring to the lives of us Christians.

Parents, as hard as it is, please don't blame yourselves when distressing incidents pop up in your kids' lives. Instead, just focus on your children's present as well as future well-being. Utilize EFT underpinned with prayer to move the problem along and release your child's anxieties and fears. Frankly, parents, the more you use EFT to help yourselves with the personal issues causing stress in your own life, the less stressed your kids will feel. You set the example for them, as with everything else in life. Do your kids the biggest favor of their young lives—pray with them, tap with them, and live for Jesus, showing your children the Way!

Had someone tapped with poor Paula about her dad's death (and, of course, EFT wasn't known back then), how different her life would have been.

As we look next at how EFT can heal behavioral issues, we'll begin with the account of a teenager's plight, whose story illustrates the connection between our emotions and our physical well-being.

6

Using EFT to Heal
Behavioral Problems

We learn worry early in our lives. Oh, it might be something that today we would find inconsequential, like not being picked for a kickball team or not understanding a formula in an upcoming math test. But at the time, worry and anxiety set in. The cognitive process learned then is instilled in our minds. Over the following decades, other problems arose that reinforced all that worry, fear, and anxiety. Each time, it seems we worry more and more, or the worry is more deeply established in our heart and mind. Finally, by middle age, we find ourselves worrying about nearly every single thing in our lives.

We can tell ourselves a million times that we have nothing to worry about, God has it all under control ("Throw all your worry on him, because he cares for you," 1 Peter 5:7), but, for some reason, that never truly reassures us or alters our internal thought process, and we continue this pattern of worry. Eventually, the guilt about our worrying begins to set in, adding to our angst.

We know in our heart it is wrong and we pray diligently to be delivered from it.

We all know God can do whatever He finds necessary in a supernatural way. Sometimes, He simply rescues us from our deep-seated worry, setting us free. Other times, it continues, like Apostle Paul's thorn (2 Corinthians 12:7–10), leaving us overburdened and sick, so we have to depend solely on Him to sustain us. God usually allows life to play out in a natural manner, within the parameters of how He created our world. God often brings in something else to assist us—a resource—and answers our prayers in practical ways. EFT is a "natural" tool He has provided for broad relief of a wide range of maladies.

Bethie's Story: Teen Compulsively Pulling out Her Hair

A friend of mine asked if I would tap with her teenage daughter who has trichotillomania, as diagnosed by her physician. This is a disorder that causes people to pull out the hair from their scalp, eyelashes, eyebrows, or other parts of the body, resulting in noticeable bald patches. Trichotillomania falls under the compulsive behavior spectrum with neural and subconscious tendencies. A strong stress, anxiety, or deep sadness component is usually intertwined within the sufferer's symptoms, too. Medication is available and the condition is treatable, but Bethie's mother prefers fewer pharmaceuticals and wanted to try tapping before making a decision to try other medical interventions.

Since we had never met and Bethie lived out of town, we opted to do our tapping session via telephone. Bethie's mom was familiar with EFT, so she instructed Bethie on the tapping points and also gave her the tapping point sheet I had e-mailed earlier. As Bethie was 15 years old, I wasn't expecting her to make the phone call, instead assuming her mom would call and then introduce Bethie to me, so I was surprised when Bethie initiated the call on her own.

Wanting her to feel comfortable with me as quickly as possible, I inquired about school and other activities to break the ice. I immediately had her begin tapping on her collarbone area as she relayed the details she felt were important about her life. I reviewed the tapping spots with her, just for good measure.

Bethie's story was familiar—typical teenage stuff including homework issues, feeling self-conscious, shy, family tension problems, caught in the middle of different groups of friends, fear of saying the wrong things, and not having anyone her age with whom she could share her Christian faith.

Bethie's SUD rating was a 7 to 8 on nearly all the issues we discussed, so we got under way. I did the Setup with Bethie in order to follow closely the instruction sheet I had given her mom. Normally, I would have just commenced tapping without the Setup because her SUD levels were quite high.

Setup:

Even though I have all this stress with home and homework, I know God loves me.

Even though I pull out my eyelashes and eyebrows pretty often without thinking about it, I know God can fix it.

Even though I know I should stop pulling my hair and I have no idea in the world why I do it, I know God can make this stop and I know He loves me anyway if I pull at my hair or if I don't.

TH: *I do this hair-pulling thing when I'm alone, usually when doing homework.*

EB: *I know I should stop but I can't.*

SE: *I'm pretty quiet and self-conscious.*

UE: *Kids like me if they get to know me, but few do.*

UN: *I feel like a pickle in the middle with my sister and my parents.*

CH: *I like my sister and her family, but my parents fight with her too much.*

CB: *A lot is expected of me at school and I can usually handle it, but it's hard sometimes.*

UA: *I feel all this tension.*

TH: *It's a lot of stress with my family.*

EB: *I don't like my looks.*

SE: *I'm pale looking.*

UE: *I know I should stop pulling my hair.*

UN: *But I can't. I don't even know I'm doing it most of the time.*

CH: *I've been doing this since I was pretty little.*

CB: *I just keep pulling at my eyelashes mostly.*

UA: *It's getting worse now.*

We did a few more rounds on these same themes.

At this point, Bethie interjected some more information. I made notes of the details and we kept tapping. She was crying. I inquired if she was okay and suggested she go get some tissues.

TH: *I have to choose between friends.*

EB: *This is hard. I'm really stuck in the middle.*

SE: *I'm the youngest and I'm simply stuck.*

UE: *They all look at me like I'm crazy.*

UN: *I feel close to God but it's hard to talk to people about Him.*

CH: *I'm the pickle in the middle* (she giggled here; humor can be helpful in bringing down the SUD level, as long as it doesn't diminish the client's feelings).

CB: *I'm scared.*

UA: *I'm really, really scared.*

TH: *I have a friend who has terrible anxiety problems.*

EB: *She is a really close personal friend.*

SE: *I try to help her too, but I can't even help myself.*

UE: *I really feel like I'm in the middle.*

UN: *I don't want to be alone.*

CH: *I'm scared. I wish I could talk to my friends about Jesus and how I feel about my Catholic faith.*

CB: *I don't want to choose anyone over anyone else.*

UA: *I'm so fearful about everything.*

As before, we did two more rounds on these issues.

At this point, Bethie began really crying. I stopped for a minute, telling her to please keep tapping on her chest if she could, and then let me know what was happening and when she wanted to continue. "I've never had a boyfriend," she told me. (Inside, I kind of wanted to giggle because she was only 15, but of course, I kept my cool and just listened!) She continued, "No one seems attracted to me. I always mess things up with my friends, especially the boys. I always say the wrong things. I don't know what to do to fix that." I inquired what she was feeling. "Embarrassed, sad, and lonely" was her answer.

TH: *I've never had a boyfriend.*

EB: *I want to feel special to someone.*

SE: *I always mess things up!*

UE: *I always, always mess stuff up with the guys!*

UN: *I don't know how to fix it.*

CH: *I'm so scared.*

CB: *I've never had a boyfriend.*

UA: *I'm so embarrassed by it all.*

TH: *I'm horribly sad about this whole situation. It will never, ever change.*

EB: *I know I will be alone forever.*

SE: *I'm so lonely.*

UE: *I'm so quiet, no one notices me at all.*

UN: *I'm stuck in the middle.*

CH: *I don't know how to fix this. How do I get out of this rut I'm in?*

CB: *I'm invisible to everyone.*

UA: *I'm terribly embarrassed to be like this. It's embarrassing to be pulling out my eyelashes, too.*

TH: *I'd like to consider the fact that maybe I could forgive myself for being this way.*

EB: *I know God understands me.*

SE: *At least He gets me, it doesn't seem like anyone else does though.*

UE: *I think I could maybe forgive myself for pulling out my eyelashes all the time.*

UN: *God forgives me.*

CH: *I forgive me.*

CB: *I'm okay with myself because God loves me.*

UA: *I forgive myself for doing this.*

At that point, we stopped to reassess the tapping sequence. Bethie reported her SUD level was down to a 2 from the original 7 or 8 at the beginning of the session. I inquired if she really did forgive herself and asked what was left in there that this was still a 2. "I feel very peaceful right now," she answered. "This won't last very long, will it? I think I can let this go."

I explained that once the neural pathways were broken (and she seemed very familiar with neural pathways from science class!), they tended to stay that way and she would begin today to build up a new neural pathway that didn't include many of the things we tapped about. So we started:

Setup:

Even though I don't believe for a minute this will last, I know God can make it last.

Even though I feel great right now and I really like what I'm feeling, there is absolutely no way this is going to last very long, I know I can count on God to make sure it does.

Even though it is impossible for this EFT thing to be this easy to make my eyelash pulling go away, I'm going to hope God makes it right and fixes this problem for me.

TH: *This won't last, but maybe God will give me a miracle. He still does miracles today, you know.*

EB: *It's simply impossible.*

SE: *This is too, too easy to fix something like this.*

UE: *It can't happen like that.*

UN: *This is absolutely impossible.*

CH: *I know this science, but no one ever told us about tapping like this to fix stuff.*

CB: *This is impossible, but my God is a God of the impossible.*

UA: *No way this is going to stay permanent.*

Bethie now reported a 0 SUD level and that she felt good. When I inquired if there was anything else she would like to tap on, she reported nothing. I explained that I would be happy to tap again in the future if something else arose that she wanted help with. Once again, I reiterated what I had told her at the session's commencement: This session was confidential; I wouldn't be telling her mom anything about it unless it was something life threatening.

Unlike many teenagers I've tapped with, mostly at the insistence of a mother, Bethie opened up easily about what was going on in her head and in her life. Most teens tell me everything is fine, fine, fine, and not much happens during their tapping sessions. Teens don't always tune in to what they're actually feeling, or share it when they do (I've parented a couple teens like that). This session had gone very well, however, and we had spent 45 productive minutes together. Her mom texted me later: "Bethie is very peaceful this afternoon, so I know the EFT helped." I told her mom to ask her to tap routinely, as I had given her enough instructions and information during our session for her to carry on by herself, while being careful not to overwhelm her.

As an EFT practitioner, I do not need to know the details of an issue in order for EFT to work. This can be useful when working with teens who don't talk or don't want to engage. I just say to them, "Think about the incident and how you feel about it while we tap."

A year after our work together, I received this e-mail from Bethie's mom:

> Bethie came downstairs, dressed in her band uniform, and came up really close to my face, saying, "Look, Mom." I answered, telling her she was pretty and looked really nice, all gussied up for

the football game. "No, *look*, Mom!" Bethie said again, and batted her eyes at me. Sure enough, I saw what she wanted me to see—her eyelashes were full again. "Mom, it worked! Sometimes, I catch myself pulling on them, but not as hard as before, more like playing with them, but mostly I just forgot I ever did that," she reported to me. Praise God, that surely does beat giving my daughter anti-anxiety pills!

What a blessing to hear this mother's joyful report of the now-healed trauma in her young daughter's life!

By harnessing the healing power of EFT, God disabled a detrimental habit that would likely have negatively impacted this girl's adult life. In the previous chapter, Amie's story was a display of outright fear. Bethie's fear took a more subtle form, but was fear based nonetheless because, underneath, she was scared that life in general wasn't really working out for her.

Tom's Story: Excessive Complaining and Anger

Here is another case in which God used EFT to short-circuit an old habit, rooted in early childhood behavior that I suspect was related to his dad, as I know the client well. What started as a child's self-defense mechanism evolved into a negative habit, interfering with the adult's life.

Tom couldn't always identify what emotion he was feeling, but he knew he was sick and tired of his wife always yelling at him for forgetting everything! I snickered to myself with this one, because I had heard the wife's complaint from nearly every woman I know. What presented itself in this session was no laughing matter, however.

Tom and I had tapped in the past, and the emotions that came up were fear, frustration, anger, and sadness. This time proved no different. Tom lay his fear and frustration on the tapping table, telling me no matter how hard he tried, he always forgot something. Then his wife got angry, yelled, and the day was ruined for both of them.

After we opened with prayer, I had Tom tune into that fear and frustration he told me was in his chest and had him tap for a minute or two, allowing his subconscious to bring to his mind the earliest event associated with this feeling that he could remember.

Sure enough, back to his childhood he went again. "Dad was always yelling at me about something. I never did anything right, so I would check and recheck everything like light switches, turning them off and on about four times. Of course, that just made Dad madder and I got yelled at even more, but I had to be sure I wouldn't burn the house down!" Tom's fear and frustration SUD level was 7, so we began the tapping.

As Tom and I tapped this round, his fear and frustration dropped, as it always had, but I wanted to take this progress a bit further. I questioned him about the light switch issue. Did he still practice that behavior in his adult life? Tom admitted that he always had, but he went further, telling me he had a few other habits that were similar, like double-checking doors and stopping the car about 5 miles down the road when leaving on vacation to make sure he had packed one thing or another. These practices also infuriated his wife.

To me, this was beginning to sound like an obsessive behavior of sorts. Tom is a very accomplished man and, to look at him, one would never suspect this behavior, but it obviously was creating some challenges in his marriage.

I asked Tom if he was willing to try something different in tapping. The fear and frustration were reduced to his usual 1 SUD level, so he was now ready to reprogram some neurons. I learned this technique from Valerie Lis, EFT-EXP (www.CoursesForLife.com; she practices secular Clinical EFT). He was agreeable to trying just about anything!

I had Tom close his eyes and imagine that he could never, ever again do anything in his life except turn light switches on and off, 24/7/365, no eating, no beer, no vacation, no sleep, nothing except turning those same switches on and off. "How do you feel about doing that?" I asked. Tom's anger and frustration went way off the chart, above a 10 SUD rating.

Taking EFT to its simplest form, we tapped "frustration" and "anger," alternating the two as we moved through the tapping points. After doing about three full rounds of tapping, Tom's SUD level dropped to 0.

I then gave opposite instructions. "Tom, you can never ever again touch a light switch to double-check it. You turn it off once and you walk away. How does that make you feel?" His answer was similar to the first question, "Frustrated." This frustration was a 9 on the SUD scale. We tapped the 9 frustration to a 1, using the same technique, alternating the words "frustration" and "light switches" on the acupressure points.

As I think about how this method works using Clinical EFT, it appears to me that neutralizing both sides of an issue by tapping on the "24/7" and "never ever" phrases, the client tends to land somewhere in the middle between the two extremes of emotion. The unbalanced, severely tipped behaviors seem to ameliorate themselves to something more controlled. In this case, it happened immediately!

I asked Tom if his anger needed to be confessed to God. He replied, "I was doing that while we tapped because I know I needed to do so and I knew you would ask."

When following up with Tom 18 months later, I inquired about the status of his light switch and door checking. He proudly related that he had not felt the need to double-check a thing since the day we tapped! Isn't EFT wondrous? To God be the glory for this tool of healing!

Jessica's Story: Short Fuse, Anger Issues

A friend of mine, to whom I taught EFT, had been tapping regularly and aggressively for a couple of years, trying to clear all of her childhood emotional and verbal abuse issues. These were heavy, deep, and, until recently, distressing memories, seriously impacting Jessica's life from that early subconscious level. Until EFT, I had no idea how much these childhood issues were driving her adult issues. She related this story to me via e-mail and I reprint it here with her permssion.

* * *

Within the past couple of days, several small events happened that showed me how much I have changed inside. I will relate one of them for you. In case you wonder why I brought this up, there's something I need you to understand: Before EFT, small things would create triggers in me big time; I'd have huge emotional blowups over pretty much nothing.

Yesterday, accidentally, I dumped half a cup of coffee all over the floor. Four years ago, I would have gone ballistic, calling myself all kinds of names, angry about the incident, yelling at everyone around me, blaming someone else for the spill, and generally ruining my entire day. Immature behavior? You bet. Over the edge for a spill? You betcha!

Now I understand where that behavior comes from—that is how my dad reacted when one of us kids spilled a glass of milk at dinner. As a kid, I thought this was how everyone reacted to incidents. He went crazy about the mess! I learned the lesson so well. He called us all kinds of names, like klutz, idiot, stupid, etc. I simply took up where he left off, calling myself the same names.

Well, lo and behold, after I cleaned up the big puddle of coffee, I realized my only reaction was "Shoot!" No swearing. No yelling. No calling myself names. No blaming anyone near me. No residual funk that often lasted for days.

I just cleaned it up with an "oh, well, stuff happens" attitude, like "normal" people do! Success! Those old, negative neural pathways have been severed, and new, less reactive ones have replaced them. Praise God! The cognitive learning has been undone.

Indeed, tapping has changed my physiology. I had essentially no reaction whatsoever.

However, I also realized for the first time in 40 years as I am writing this, the stabbing, tightening cringe I felt in my heart when I pictured that white milk slowly spreading all over the table, under the serving bowls, plates, butter dish, and, absolutely worst of all, down the crack in the table where the extension leaves touched. Mom would then get into the yelling, name-calling act, too, because she would have to take the table apart to clean that mess.

This recovered memory could well be the last aspect of healing this old behavior. I'm so excited. I will tap this "cringing" memory away, releasing it and letting it go forever, too. I love happy endings.

I like this new me better. I'm more in control. Spilled coffee is not worth raising my cortisol level for 2 days! Elevated cortisol levels and blood pressure do not serve my physical health. [See Chapter 2 for an explanation of cortisol.]

Through EFT, God has changed behaviors that I have tried all my life to change. EFT gave me the boost to accomplish what my conscious mind could not do alone. And I tried for years to teach myself to stop screaming about everything, to no avail. I'm so grateful to God for this precious gift, literally this gift of peace and restoration.

* * *

Thank you, Jessica, for sharing your story. This is a great illustration of how EFT works. One session at a time, we clean up our past traumas, large and small. Sooner or later, if persistence is applied, God just uses this process to level us out. Those events that once triggered us simply no longer do so. There are so many more important things in life for us to enjoy versus being enslaved to constant triggers by the same old stuff. And it is just stuff. All that stuff carries useless, inconsequential memories that no longer contribute anything worthwhile to our current stage of life. God really does want you to be happy and joyful—and EFT is such a worthwhile tool to help you achieve that goal.

Thomas's Story: Needing to Get Even

Thomas came to me for help with his marital issues. As much as he tried to be kind and thoughtful to his wife, his resolve vanished after about 2 weeks, meaning he then had to "start all over again," as he explained it. His childhood had been marked by significant verbal abuse from as early as he could remember. We had tapped on many of these early issues, but he claimed something was still sticking in his craw over the issue of "getting even" with his wife when she pointed out any household problems.

He knew his behavior was wrong, but he just couldn't seem to stop saying or doing hurtful things on purpose. Thomas is a Christian, so as we have previously, we tackled this issue from a Christian tapping perspective.

We began with a general Setup:

Even though I have no idea what is bugging me, something is stuck and I can't identify it, I know God can show me what it is.

Even though I know it revolves around the revenge issue with my wife, it's stuck and I can't seem to pull it out, I know God can fix it.

Even though something is stuck in there around my wife and I can't seem to do better than a couple of weeks of niceness before I falter and get vengeful, I know God can figure this all out for me.

TH: *I'm vengeful.*

EB: *It's killing my marriage.*

SE: *This revenge gets me all off track.*

UE: *I can only be nice for a couple of weeks and then I revert to my old behavior.*

UN: *I'll show her.*

CH: *I'm off track.*

CB: *I'm vengeful and I don't know why.*

UA: *This is wrecking my marriage.*

We did a round or two of these reminders when I received inspiration from the Holy Spirit to ask a few more questions.

"What does vengefulness look like to you, Thomas?" I asked. "A big sign, with big red letters," he replied. "What letters?" I asked. He spelled out "V-E-N-G-E-A-N-C-E." "Neon letters," I asked? "Yes, a flashing red neon sign with VENGEANCE written on it," he answered. "Where is the sign located? I inquired. "On a big hill, like the Hollywood sign," Thomas replied.

As he had rated the intensity as a 10 on the SUD scale at the start of our tapping, I went right back into Reminder Phrases:

TH: *Big red neon sign.*

EB: *It's flashing "vengeance." Jesus, help me.*

SE: *It's bright red and just keeps flashing at me.*

UE: *Vengeance, vengeance, vengeance.*

UN: *It just won't stop flashing.*

CH: *I've gotten off the track and now this sign is flashing at me.*

CB: *Vengeance. Jesus, please forgive me. I'm vengeful.*

UA: *It's bright red, like a warning light.*

I asked Thomas if he would like to turn off the sign. He indicated he surely would. I had him close his eyes, focusing on the big red flashing neon vengeance sign. I asked him if he could follow the electric cord to its source in order to pull it out and turn it off. "There is no cord," Thomas replied, "It's a battery." "Okay, can you find the batteries?" I asked. "Yes, they're in a box underneath the flashing sign," he said. I asked if he wanted to, could he remove the batteries powering the sign. "No, the box has a switch," he answered. "A toggle switch?" I wanted to know. "Yes, a toggle," he told me. I again asked if he wanted to turn this bright sign off. An emphatic "Yes!" was his reply. I inquired if he could reach it because he had mentioned that the box was in an odd place. "Yes, it's really low, but I can get at it," he said. I asked if he had his finger on the switch yet. "Yes, my finger is right there." I told him to take his time but let me know when he had turned off the vengeance sign. A few minutes later, he announced, "I flipped it off." "For sure it is off now, right?" I wanted to know. He said yes.

Thomas kept tapping throughout this question-and-answer sequence. His eyes were closed as he focused on the bright flashing neon sign his subconscious had brought forth to him.

I asked him how he felt now that the toggle switch to the vengeance sign had been turned off. "Relieved. That was really hard to turn off. I didn't want to do it. That took a while to make myself flip that switch," Thomas replied. "How relieved are you?" I asked. "Relieved enough now that it is gone that I want to walk back down the hill and away from that sign. I never want it turned on again. Ever," he answered.

I told Thomas to go ahead and start back down the hill away from the now darkened sign.

We tapped another round:

TH: *The neon sign is off. I like it this way.*

EB: *It's out. I want it to stay off.*

SE: *I don't have to look at it any longer.*

UE: *God, I'm so sorry for my sin of vengefulness.*

UN: *I repent of it. It was wrong to do, but I could never stop myself.*

CH: *Please forgive me, Jesus.*

CB: *Help me never to do it again.*

UA: *Please help me never to do that again.*

I gave Thomas "homework," asking him to tap a couple of times a day for the next 3 to 4 weeks. He was to turn around and look up that "Hollywood" hill at the darkened red neon vengeful sign, telling himself, "I turned it off and I like it that way." He agreed to do so.

Thomas reported at the end of this tapping session that his 10 SUD level had dropped to a 0 and he felt God's forgiveness for what he had done. He also mentioned that he felt confident that the "vengeance" part of his life that had been with him from childhood was now gone. We prayed the "I'll stick it to my wife" attitude was now permanently gone, a greatly improved, positive move toward marital harmony!

I recently checked in with Thomas, about 18 months after this tapping session addressing his need to get revenge and "show his wife," and he reported the problem was still completely gone. In fact, it was so completely dissipated that when he mentally envisioned looking up where the "vengeance" sign on Hollywood hill was, the sign had disappeared from sight. Praise God!

As illustrated by Thomas's successful session, EFT can renew your moral base no matter what age you are, no matter what type of physical or emotional background you have ("Do not conform to the pattern of this world, but be transformed by the renewing of your mind. Then you will be able to test and approve what God's will is—his good, pleasing and perfect will," Romans 12:2). God has implanted in us the process of neuroplasticity to accomplish the unlearning of sinful habits and desires, releasing negative emotions, and replacing them with positive thoughts and more God-pleasing behaviors. God would have us live a life of love and grace, in thankfulness for what was done for us by Jesus on the Cross. A life such as this can then be used more fully to minister to others and edify God. An abundant and healed life can flow out to those around the person who has healed in this way. Neuroplasticity means we can learn anything new, at any age. In fact, "Old dogs can learn new tricks," to reverse the old adage. Science has proven it!

EFT for Christians: The Great Equalizer

Why should Christians tap? Because EFT is the great equalizer. This personal tool, which can so simply be practiced in private, has the power to level out all our emotions, leaving us on a smoother path, with fewer ups and downs when confronting life's challenges. Plus EFT releases us from old emotional hurts and enduring painful memories and their ongoing taint on our lives.

As you continue EFT tapping, you will find God clearing your mind of those things that make you fearful, distressed, and anxious—including feelings of unworthiness or being unloved. We all have these, each of us with our own version. As a result of this emotional clearing, you will find yourself in a more prayerful, grateful mode.

It's like being more in the presence of Jesus all the time. You will actually feel God! God hasn't changed, but you have. He has always been right beside you, but you and I have been weighed down by a toxic emotional cloud pressing on our old wounds. We've been burdened and buried in our own distress. Satan, of course, likes it when we are in such a state because we become more vulnerable and weak, and numb to our feelings. I Peter 5:8 reads, "The devil prowls around like a roaring lion looking for someone to devour."

I notice that being sick tends to trigger a certain habit of mine. I wonder if this rings any bells with you. When I'm feeling miserable, I cry out to God in a childlike manner, complaining away, and begging Him to make me better. I don't have the ambition or the wherewithal to have a meaningful conversation with Him in prayer. I just whine, assuming I'm the only miserable person on the face of the Earth. I don't really have to be all that sick either; a simple cold is enough ammunition for me to mope to my heavenly Father. But I'm not actually feeling Him when I'm whining. I'm acting very much like a 2-year-old, hoping to get my way with my Father, asking Him to make me better.

I want to know God, but I also want to feel Him. I want to feel Him all around me, in everything I do. I can't feel God when my life is full of emotional hang-ups. My anger, fear, disappointment, and disgust get in my way spiritually, just as feeling physically unwell does. During those times, I can't think, my emotions overwhelm and preoccupy me. I often wonder if I'm not violating the First Commandment, selfishly setting myself up as my own god when I react this way!

EFT is a fantastic and gentle way to move those feelings and events aside and out of the way in your walk with your Savior. We are told we sadden Him with our sins. Take the time while tapping to confess those sins that you know in your heart hurt Him.

EFT resensitizes you to hear the Holy Spirit's voice clearly. All the numbness and busyness we've adopted in life makes it extremely difficult to listen to Him. As we tap and pray, our brain waves drop down into the alpha and theta ranges and out of that overactive, rattling, and noisy beta state. The great Christian meditators are operating in these lowered brain waves when they commune deeply with God. Jesus' own brain likely dropped into those lowered wave states when He privately communed with His Father.

EFT also quiets the chatter and negative self-talk in which we all unconsciously engage. I had a ton of that going on nearly constantly before discovering EFT. This inner "noise" is particularly prevalent in those who come from an abusive background. A smart woman once told me that when the abusers stop abusing us, or we are out of their reach, we continue to abuse ourselves in the exact same way they did, as we learned the pattern from them. We tell ourselves we are no good, or stupid, or ugly, or worthless. Whatever your poison, you just keep drinking it from the well of your own subconscious. By using

EFT, however, you can reprogram and neutralize these patterns and stop the negative self-talk once and for all.

Moving along all these little "puzzle pieces" delivers to us the result we desire—peace of mind. Taking a walk is now a pleasant experience. My mind is no longer racing, rerunning all those old emotional movies from my past I once played over and over again. And that is all the internal mind chatter is—old movies. There is a saying that goes like this: To the conscious mind, a memory is only a memory, but to the subconscious mind it is a current event. (I wish I knew who said it so I could give them proper credit, but, sadly, I don't.) Until that event is unplugged and dismissed via tapping, it will just keep playing in an endless loop. And it will also continue to cause you emotional and possibly physical grief as a result.

So now you can apply the soothing ointment of EFT to old memories and undo them, eliminating the self-deprecating chatter that is upsetting everything in your life. Take that step of faith and allow God to heal you. Simply use the techniques in this book. Begin *today!*

Remember Psalm 46:10, "Be still and know that I am God," and "All the lands are at rest and at peace; they break into singing" (Isaiah 14:7).

7

Using EFT to Heal
Physical Pain

In learning about EFT, we discover that people suffering from physical ailments often have emotional issues from their past stored in their "body mind" (the late Dr. Candace Pert credits acupuncturist Diane Connelly as the person who coined this term). The newly unlocked physiology research of the last two decades proves beyond a shadow of a doubt that memories aren't stored in the brain but are stored somewhere in the body, whether in the muscles, organs, tissues, bones, or other body part. Dr. Pert states, "Mind doesn't dominate body, it becomes body—body and mind are one. I see the whole process of communication we have demonstrated, the flow of information throughout the whole organism, as evidence that the body is the actual outward manifestation, in physical space, of the mind" (Pert, 1997, p. 187).

Let's take a look at a number of examples of this mind-body connection from my case history files.

Judy's Story: Chronic Foot Pain

My friend Judy sent me a text relating to something else, but in the course of the digital conversation, she mentioned her foot was killing her, making walking an issue. She had spent nearly $200 on new shoes and supports but she wasn't sure any of these resources were helping. She wondered if perhaps tapping might help bring her some relief and I readily agreed to try.

As usual, I had Judy begin tapping as we talked through her foot problem and we opened the session with prayer:

"Holy Spirit, sit here with Judy and I as we tap through this foot problem that has arisen for her. We ask for your healing power to come upon both of us. Whisper in our ears what You know about this situation that we need to hear to move this pain along. You are the Great Healer so please help us as we tap. In Jesus' name, we pray."

Judy told me she had been dealing with this pain for almost a year. She had a callus on the side of her right foot, and now she noticed she had calluses on the balls of both feet as well. It was really making walking painful for her.

She continued by telling me she had offered to pet-sit a neighbor's dog, doing this as a "good Samaritan," but the dog had gotten out of the yard. She had duly chased it for three blocks, running on her hurting feet. "My feet were killing me when I finally caught that dog," she said.

I asked her to tell me more specifics about her foot pain. "It feels like pressure on my foot, like I have a stone in my shoe. It sends shooting and throbbing pain through the calluses. Calluses are excess skin in the way. They are hard and uncomfortable," she said.

When asked, "Does this remind you of anything?" Judy replied, "Yeah, my age! I'm having a really hard time letting go of Cindy [her youngest daughter]. In many ways, I'm living my life through hers. Hers is much more exciting than mine. Mine is ending and hers is just beginning. I cannot take care of Mom if I can't walk. I never did much of anything when I was Cindy's age because Dad wouldn't let me. I had to come right home from school to help Mom, or I had to go right to work once I had a job."

I inquired as to how all of that made her feel. Judy replied, "I have all these regrets about how I lived my life when I was Cindy's age. I could have done so much, but I didn't." She indicated she felt "sadness" and "regret" on those issues. Sadness held a SUD level of 10 and the regret was at 7 or 8.

As we tapped on the sadness and the regret, Judy mentioned, "I'm 58 years old, and I have no feet." She continued, "I need to leave Cindy alone, but I can't." Judy told me a bit more of what was going on with her as she tapped.

"Cindy has a nice male friend. I think he likes her more than she likes him, but they get along and he's a responsible guy. I keep checking on everything Cindy does. I ask her a million questions about where they went and what they did. I'm a little wacko about it all. I even go onto AT&T to check out how much Cindy is texting him. I'm driving my daughter crazy. The harder I hold on, the more I realize I could drive her away. This is my last chance to get it right with my kids. Cindy will run away if I don't stop," Judy told me.

That was a mouthful! When asked what emotion all that elicited, she replied, "Fear."

"Fear of what exactly?" I asked. "Fear that my kids will desert me. Cindy is trying to get out of the house. I have three sons and none of them call me. If I fell off the face of the earth, would they even notice? I was number five in my family, and I remember always wondering how I was going to get out. I was the youngest girl, so who would take care of Mom and Dad when they were old? This all really hits a nerve," she told me.

I inquired as to how her feet were doing. "Interestingly," she replied, "while talking about all this, I have shooting pain up the side of my right foot where that callus is."

As this was a phone session, I could smile to myself as I realized Judy had no idea how much emotion she had stuffed into her feet!

We tapped for a while on the fear of her kids deserting her, and Cindy's imminent departure in the fall for college. I threw in a wee bit of the former regret and sadness, too, for good measure.

Judy indicated she now felt peaceful and much better, with the shooting pains in her feet subsiding. Her SUD levels were all down to 0, but I wanted to test it all a bit more.

I asked Judy to look into her feet and ask them if they wanted to tell her anything else. She kind of giggled and told me, "I forgot this until now. You know, I have an extra bone in both feet. The doctor told me that surgery could fix them, but if they weren't bothering me he recommended leaving them alone. He said the extra bone wouldn't bother me when I was a kid, but said wait until I get older, as then it will."

"Well, the doctor appears to have set you up for this, didn't he?" I answered. She retorted with, "I bet he did, because I have thought about that ever since!"

As an EFT practitioner, it is often important to ask a client what a doctor said about the physical problem being addressed by tapping because the subconscious will pick up on all those statements and make them its own, causing whatever opinion was expressed (especially by an authority figure) to manifest physically because the subconscious thinks that is what we want—in other words, we ultimately adopt what the doctor says as "our truth." I often tap all the emotions around a doctor's visit and a doctor's specific words.

Curiously, I wanted to know the doctor's name. "Dr. Order" came the answer.

We tapped about Dr. Order telling Judy that her feet would give her problems when she "got older."

Before long, Judy was laughing her head off over the whole feet issue, telling me, "I had no idea that was all involved in this. I've been wanting to call you, but I figured you'd think I was nuts wanting to tap on this."

I later e-mailed Judy to point out all the different words she used regarding her feet: Running, walking, can't walk, no feet, barefoot, driving, run away, trying to get out, nerve, bone, and probably others I can no longer recall.

Judy is a Christian client, so through much of this session we prayed as we tapped. As we do that, the client and I feel we are tapping right into God's divine healing power. I lead the client by saying, "Oh, Lord, I feel all this regret," or "Oh, Lord, that pain in my foot is unbearable at times, just like the pain you bore on the Cross for me was totally unbearable." I never tap any two cases alike, so with some cases, I use a lot of prayer; with other cases, I use less. It's determined completely by how comfortable the client is with this method.

When I tap with non-Christian clients, I use no references to God. We just tap in the manner of Clinical EFT. Usually, I know from the client when the appointment is made whether she or he has contacted me because I offer Christian EFT. Clients tend to make it clear what they want. It is my job as an EFT practitioner to tap according to what best suits them, as it's their healing session.

Clients tend to yawn, laugh, or sigh when the energy around their issue is released. In Judy's case, she laughed and laughed.

I instructed her to pay attention though as there could still be more issues stuffed into those feet of hers, and if so, she could tap on them herself, or call me to help her do so.

I received an e-mail from her a few days later, telling me much of her foot pain had resolved and she was feeling a whole lot better. Six months later, her foot pain remains in abeyance, and she recently e-mailed me: "I haven't finished reading what you wrote about my foot. I have been doing so much running." To which I can only say with thanksgiving, "Amen, Lord!"

Beverly's Story: Severe Migraine Headaches

Beverly and I planned an EFT phone session for a beautiful Wednesday afternoon. We talked pleasantries for a few minutes, as I have known Beverly for years. "I'm sorting stuff, but my migraine pain is much less, although sometimes bright lights still trigger a small one. We want to go to camp in a few days, but Greg is not helping me get any of this work done at all. I don't know what he is doing outside all the time. It all just makes me so angry," she began. "Not only do I not know what he is doing outside, he gave the kids some more of our retirement money. What he wants is not what I want. This has to stop."

When I could get a word in edgewise, I asked her to hang onto those thoughts and could we please just say a word of prayer before we got under way. This might appear disrespectful to some, but Beverly and I have been friends forever, and I know that, like me, she is a devout Christian. God is the center of it all, no matter what we are feeling.

Beverly apologized for not thinking of that before she started "ranting and raving." We then prayed.

I asked her what she was feeling at this moment along with that anger toward Greg. Her answer was, "My back is really hurting me right now. I'm hurt, disgusted, frustrated, and angry, all wrapped up into one."

Beverly knows the EFT drill, so she told me the back pain was at a SUD level of 3 or 4, and the emotions were at 7.

To get her back on track, I inquired to whom Greg had given the money. "The youngest [Jennifer]" was her answer. "We have given them money before and they never pay it back. I'll never see a nickel of it again and I wish Greg would just stop. They have to figure this out on their own. I can't keep bailing them out all the time. Greg is always bragging about our money, so I guess the kids think we are swimming in it, but we aren't. I wish he would stop that, too," she told me. "No one showed up here with anything for Mother's Day. Do they think that is acceptable? And Jennifer defriended me on Facebook last summer. What was that all about? I keep her kids for her all the time. I'm sick and tired of it all. I'm disgusted with myself for letting her do this to me. Our oldest daughter, Stephanie, hasn't been to our house since New Year's Day. It would have been nice had she simply phoned me on Mother's Day."

Beverly finally took a breath, and I suggested, "Let's do a bit of some specific tapping on all that you just told me. Is your anger still a 7?" She said no, it was a 10, adding, "I'm so mad at them all. Who do they think I am?"

I'm so very angry. I've had it with them all. Who do they think I am?

I'm so very angry, Lord, I could just scream right now.

I'm disgusted with myself because I let them all walk all over me.

I'm so angry.

All this frustration. No one seems to care what I think or want.

I'm so frustrated.

Greg is always bragging about our money, and then he gives it all away to the girls.

Jennifer defriended me on Facebook. How dare she do that? I'm her mother!

All this back pain. All I do is cook and clean. No one helps me.

I'm sick and tired of moving furniture to make some room in this house for something I want.

I'm so angry at them all.

Why can't someone act like I matter a little bit?

We continued for about six or seven rounds with statements similar to these. I could hear Beverly's voice soften and quiet down. I knew something had changed.

She had switched aspects here, and told me a story about her oldest granddaughter's teacher who was accused of sexual harassment and how concerned she was over that. "It doesn't seem to bother Jennifer that something is going on with her daughter. The state police interviewed the child. My granddaughter ended up in the hospital for 5 days with a breathing problem after that. I don't know what is going on."

Once again Beverly switched events when I asked her if the back pain reminded her of anything. "Yes, I had terrible back pain when I was pregnant with Jennifer. We lived on the second story of a house and I could barely make it up those steps. I couldn't wait for that pregnancy to be over," she explained. I asked how she felt now about that back pain. "I'm frustrated about it because I think that was the beginning of my back pain now," she answered. Her frustration was a 6 on the SUD scale.

We tapped that frustration down to a 0.

I asked what else was in her back pain. She tapped on the eyebrow point for a minute and said, "I'm still so angry at Greg. He bought an old golf cart so he can putter around the property, and my car has 180,000 miles on it. Doesn't he think that money would be better spent replacing that car? And he buys all this dumb little stuff at the store on our credit card, and then I get a surprise at the end of the month when I go to pay it. I'm so angry with him. He doesn't think."

We tapped the SUD 9 anger down to a 1.

I asked Beverly to go in and inquire of her back pain if it had anything else to say.

"No, it says we are done for today."

Knowing this was a pretty exhausting session, intensive as it was, I thought that adding some of my Scripture tapping protocols to the end of the session might be in order.

I chose the following:

"I am blessed with all spiritual blessing in heavenly places in Christ." (Eph. 1:3)

"I am chosen by You, my Father, and I'm holy and without blame." (Eph. 1:4)

"I am Your child according to the good pleasures of Your Holy Will." (Eph. 1:5)

"I am redeemed through the Blood of Jesus." (Eph. 1:7)

"I am His heir." (Eph. 1:11)

"I have a spirit of wisdom and revelation in the knowledge of Christ." (Eph. 1:17)

"I am saved by Your Grace." (Eph. 2:5)

"I am of Your household; I am a citizen of heaven." (Eph. 2:19)

"I am strengthened with might by Your Spirit." (Eph. 3:16)

"I am rooted and grounded in God's love." (Eph. 3:17)

"I am more than a conqueror in Christ." (Rom. 8:37)

"I am an overcomer in Jesus." (Rev. 12:11)

"I am free in Christ." (John 8:36)

"I am victorious in Jesus' Resurrection." (1 John 5:4)

"Jesus is Lord over my spirit, body, soul, and mind." (Phil. 2:9-11)

For all of those who like positive tapping, I find there is nothing better for Christians than tapping Scripture.

Beverly indicated that she felt very relieved after tapping these verses.

What were Beverly and I doing here? We were smoothing off all those rough edges of life with tapping. Beverly's case differs little from anyone else's. Carrying around all her baggage is not living abundantly, as Jesus has called us to do. Most people understand the connection between stress, anxiety, and tight muscles. We get angry and our jaw clenches. We feel it for days.

Remember, when these heavy emotions come up or you stew for days or weeks over some incident, the whole inside of your body is doing exactly what your jaw or shoulders are doing (and more!) —tightening up. The stress hormone levels rise, causing all kinds of internal havoc to the body. At a minimum, EFT "de-stresses us," but God created tapping to do far more than that for us.

Carol's Story: Severe Allergies

Carol came to me complaining of horrible allergies. "They are driving me totally nuts," she said. "I don't know what else to do. I take so, so many antihistamines a day and still get no relief." She knew I was "doing something new" and decided she'd ask me if I could try it on her problem. I've known Carol for years and her allergies were indeed out of control.

I asked when her allergies started, as she has had allergies for the 25 years I've known her. She had to think awhile on this question. Finally, she told me she'd had no allergies through college, meaning they had to have started in early adulthood following her graduation.

On the SUD scale of 0 to 10, Carol reported her allergy discomfort was 8 or higher. I decided to tap generally on the allergies and see where EFT took us.

Setup:

Even though these allergies are driving me nuts, God loves me completely.

Even though it seems like I eat a bottle of allergy pills a day and get no relief, I'm praying God has a better idea than this.

Even though I feel these allergies run my life and not the other way around, I'd rather my Savior run my life, not my allergies.

We tapped on:

These allergies.

I'm sick of all these allergies.

The allergies are running my life.

These allergies are ruining my life.

All I do is eat one pill after another and I still get absolutely no relief.

These allergies are maddening to me.

All these annoying allergies.

I hate these allergies.

I had informed Carol (as I do all my clients) that if my words did not ring true or did not touch her emotionally to ignore them or change the words to make the session more meaningful to her. In order to make EFT more effective, she needed to feel the emotion of the words being said. The words needed to have an impact on her.

We tapped through the body and head points effectively twice with Carol following my lead. I stopped her and asked her what she was thinking and feeling.

Carol began telling me about her mother's death. Her mom had been diagnosed with breast cancer a year or two after Carol's college graduation. Carol seemed extremely dependent emotionally on her mom. Mom had chosen Valley of the Good Shepherd as her hospice. This was back in the days when doctors told patients to smoke so as to "calm their nerves" and Carol's mom dutifully bought a pack of cigarettes to calm her anxiety. Carol hated the fact that her mother took up smoking while she was dying of cancer. The cigarette smoke smelled bad to Carol and irritated her eyes.

We tapped on the cigarette smoking while Mom was dying of breast cancer, which was an 8 on the SUD scale:

> *I hated that cigarette smoke.*
>
> *It was bad enough Mom had breast cancer, but now she was taking up smoking, too.*
>
> *It smelled terrible. I hate cigarette smoke to this day. It sets my allergies off.*
>
> *That smoke made my eyes water.*
>
> *All I can remember is the big cloud of smoke over Mom's bed.*
>
> *I hated that cigarette smoke.*
>
> *My eyes burned like crazy.*

I totally detested that awful cigarette smoke, stinking stuff.

Once again, I did two rounds of tapping on the smoking issue. I could see a shift of some kind in Carol's eyes. She just looked like her thoughts were far away. Stopping, I asked what had just happened and whether the SUD level had come down at all. It had come down to a 4, but now Carol talked of the smothering feeling she had a week or two after the smoking issue commenced, when they were called back to the hospice about midnight because her mom had taken "a turn for the worse." When I asked for her SUD level on the smothering issue, she said it was a 7. SUD levels rise as aspects change. The client drops down fairly low, but then some other triggering detail of the event comes to mind, and the SUD level goes right back up again, often nearing 10.

We started the tapping once again:

They called us back because Mom wasn't doing too well.

She was moaning in pain.

Her breathing was awful.

She looked blue.

It was time for God to take her home to heaven. This is no way to live.

All I could smell was the cigarette smoke and suddenly I didn't feel I could breathe either.

I felt like I was smothering and gasping for air just like Mom.

Is this what it's like to die? Did both of us have to smother before we went to heaven?

This is my Mom. This is terrible. She really is dying. My God, I'm so scared!

Again, we tapped three rounds on the breathing issues, as tears were running down Carol's cheeks. I could see this was having a huge impact on her. We stopped to evaluate what was going on. The SUD level had come down to a 2 after being a 5. Her tears stopped. When I asked her how she felt overall, she told me she felt lighter. It "felt good to get this off my chest, but I remember Mom in the hospital after the cancer surgery hooked up to all those tubes with blood on the bandages. I just about fainted. I had to go outside the room to get some air. I was scared."

Carol rated this issue a 6. The aspect changed again to "scared." We returned to tapping. I didn't do any further Setups because Carol had an obvious emotional connection to these issues. I have found that, when an emotional connection to an issue is obviously present, there is usually no need to do the tapping Setup, so I went right into tapping on the new aspect of the event of her mother dying:

I am scared.

Mom was hooked up to all those tubes.

There were so many tubes.

The blood is everywhere. Why hasn't someone cleaned up this mess?

I can't get my breath. I need some air.

I feel like I'm going to faint. I can't do this!

Why is no one doing anything for her?

I don't know if I can stay here and witness this.

I'm so scared. God, please help us.

At this point, I asked Carol if there was another time in her life when she felt like passing out. After thinking for a few minutes, Carol brought up a surgery of her mom's when Carol was 10 or 12 years old. This was a hysterectomy performed at St. Luke's Medical Center. Her mother didn't want Carol home with her dad and older brother because they wouldn't take good enough care of her. "Who would have done my hair for school?" Carol recalls her mother's reasoning. "So Mom sent me to Auntie Mabel and Uncle George's for the 2 weeks. I didn't really like it there even though Auntie Mabel took me everywhere on the street car." Carol remembered nearly fainting at the sight of blood that time, too, when she went to visit her mom in the hospital. The hysterectomy blood issue was another 6 on the SUD scale.

We tapped:

There was too much blood for me to handle.

I was scared.

I was only 12. Why did they make me look at that?

I didn't want to go to Auntie Mabel's.

I wanted my mom, and I still want my mom.

No one told me anything. I guess they figured I was too young.

What was going on? I'm scared. I can't breathe. I'm going to faint. This is too much!

When was Mom coming home again?

Once again I noticed a shift. I asked Carol what she was thinking. "Mom didn't come home that last time. She died," Carol said, and then more crying started. "I miss her so much. No one could replace Mom. She was the center of our family." I asked if I could tap on her and she said yes.

I told Carol to tell the story of her mom's death and stop telling it when she felt any emotion rise, and we would tap then on the issue or particular detail that was especially painful for her to recall. I also told her I would tap on her head and face if she could not continue at any point.

Carol returned to the memory of the hospice the night her mom died. They were bedded down in the waiting room, not being permitted to stay in the room with her dying mother. Another aspect change happened here. We tapped:

We weren't allowed to stay with Mom.

They made us go to another room. Lord, why can't I be there? You might take her soon.

I didn't want to go to sleep, I wanted to be with Mother.

They gave us blankets and told us to stay in the waiting room.

The nurses would call us if they thought we were needed.

I wasn't allowed in her room.

No one cared if we wanted to be in her room.

Mom was dying. I wanted to be with her for what time she had left and no one cared.

This issue had begun at an 8. After two rounds of tapping, it was down to a 4. We did two more rounds, which brought it down to a 2.

Carol did not tell me about the actual death, but went right to the funeral, which obviously had a great impact on her. "Mom didn't want a big get-together, but there was one anyway. I felt guilty about that, but it wasn't under my control." Carol felt this was a 5 on the SUD scale. So we tapped:

Mom wanted a quiet funeral. She was in heaven. She wasn't here anyway.

She didn't want a big get-together.

It was a closed casket. At least, they listened to that part.

All the guilt that we didn't listen to what Mom wanted. I tried to tell Dad.

Mom hated to be in the middle of things. She let God have that job.

I feel bad we didn't do as she asked.

I didn't like this at all.

Everyone did as they wanted. No one listened to what Mom wanted.

Carol's face changed a bit, lightening up, so I asked her SUD rating now. It was a 1, and Carol continued her story: "No one at all showed up from my work for the funeral. No one cared enough to come." Carol rated this a 6 on the SUD scale.

We tapped:

> *No one cared.*
>
> *No one cared enough to show up. I almost felt like God wasn't around either.*
>
> *Mom wanted to be insignificant.*
>
> *I felt insignificant, since no one from work came to the funeral.*
>
> *Where is everyone? God, are you here?*
>
> *No one cares.*
>
> *Can't someone take some time for me?*
>
> *No one cares.*

One round of tapping dropped the SUD level to a 2. Carol continued by relating that in the procession to the front of the church just before the funeral service started, she was so upset that her older brother and sister were practically holding her up as she walked. "I was crying really hard," she said. "Then someone near the front leaned over and said to me, 'Stop crying. You are acting like a heathen.'" I asked her what she did then. Carol said, "I sniffled a bit more, stood up straight, and bucked up, even though we were in the front row with everyone staring at us, listening to 'Abide with Me,' which I can't play on the organ for any funerals now without crying."

We tapped. Carol was weeping again, as the heathen issue was a 9 SUD score and being in the front row getting stared at, conspicuously, everything her mom hated, was at an 8.

> *I was really crying hard.*
>
> *Mom was dead. She went to heaven and I'm in front of all these people without her.*
>
> *This was it. Her funeral is here.*
>
> *I'd never see her again.*
>
> *John and Amy were holding me up as we walked.*
>
> *I could barely stand this. What was I going to do without Mom here?*
>
> *Stop crying, you heathen, that lady said.*
>
> *You're weak.*

Twice through with head and body tapping only brought this down to a SUD level of 6, so we kept going:

> *You are acting like you have no hope. Your mom is in heaven.*
>
> *Why are you crying?*
>
> *Stop crying.*
>
> *Are you a baby?*
>
> *Everyone is staring at you.*
>
> *Abide with me. God, come abide with me now.*
>
> *Stop crying.*
>
> *Stop crying. You must be a heathen for crying. Don't you believe in heaven? Why are people so mean?*

We tapped on this for probably 10 minutes, back and forth, on all the details, until her crying stopped and the

SUD level came down to between 1 and 2. After her Dad died a few years later, Carol remembered another person telling her, "You are now an orphan." The orphan issue was a 6. Aspect change after aspect change arrived fairly quickly. Praise God, what a way to remove the emotional pain from a very difficult memory!

We tapped:

> *You are an orphan.*
>
> *Everyone is now gone.*
>
> *You are alone.*
>
> *No one cares.*
>
> *You are now an orphan.*
>
> *Mom and Dad are dead.*
>
> *I'm an orphan.*
>
> *I'm an orphan.*

Carol then changed the words for the next two rounds to: *"I am no longer an orphan, I'm adopted by God."* Her face changed to a slight smile and the enthusiasm that I know to be Carol's essence slowly returned. I could see her demeanor lighten as the session progressed and finally she broke into a big grin, telling me, "Yeah, I'm adopted by God. He tells me so in His Word." This issue melted away to a 0.

I wanted to get back to the initial issue of her allergies before this long session ended, so I asked Carol to think about her allergies once again by answering this question for me: "Did you cry again about your mom after that person in church told you to 'stop crying like a heathen'?" She thought awhile, then said, "Not really."

The Holy Spirit gave me an idea (intuition) and I asked if she thought the allergies and the grief were related in any way. She again thought awhile and finally answered, "None that I can think of, although the timing is close."

I've known Carol for many, many years, so I felt enough of a rapport to help her out a bit here, something I might not do in other situations. I asked her to think about this question: "Do you think it possible, knowing what I have told you about EFT and the articles you have read, that the tears of grief were prematurely stopped, but your subconscious is still crying for your mom in particular, and maybe your dad, too, and it's manifesting as a runny nose and watery eyes and being attributed to allergies?"

She looked puzzled, then answered, "I never thought of that! Maybe they do have something to do with each other!" I told her I thought the they might indeed be related and suggested we meet again soon to work on her specific allergies if she wanted, or she could do the tapping on them herself.

Just for good measure, before we quit the entire story regarding the funeral, I asked Carol to recount the event once again to me, starting at the point before the family was called to the hospice that last night. Carol did so, emotionless, without a tear shed, telling me, "It was a bummer to me Mom died when I was so young, but the whole thing has helped me grow and I understand how others feel when they have a loved one die. I won't be like that person who told me to quit crying. They had no clue. I know Mom's in heaven and I will see her again someday."

I was pleased with this session, as it had been comprehensive. We started with one issue and ended up with her mom's death as Carol's real core issue.

As a follow-up a month later, Carol reported that her spring allergies had settled down immensely and she had stopped all Benadryl and Claritin without any more problems. She was extremely pleased. God be praised!

I've since asked Carol about her allergies and she reports they have not reared their head again. She subsequently tapped on her food allergies and they are completely gone now as well. Praise God! He is amazing! She'd developed many food allergies over the years, to the point that she had begun to wonder how many foods would be left for her to eat.

For years, Carol had been under a doctor's care, getting allergy testing and many rounds of desensitizing shots, all to no avail. Her case clearly shows the connection between underlying emotional issues and their physical manifestations. (Remember, as always, when suffering from a physical problem, please consult a medical doctor as needed prior to using EFT.)

Carol further noted that she now routinely plays the song "Abide with Me" at funerals, singing along with the organ, without any physiological reaction. I asked her to read this case study and pay particular attention to her body as she did, watching for any remnant signs of emotion. She reported happily that there were none!

Carol had carried these painful memories around for nearly 40 years. Her increasingly annoying allergies grew yearly in depth and breadth, making her feel sick all the time. Like many of us, she had no idea that her mother's death had any connection to her physical maladies.

The Power of the Subconscious

Accessing the subconscious memory is the key to uncovering the connections between the emotions and a physical condition. As we tap, EFT accesses it by dropping us into the lower alpha and theta brain states. While in those lower brain wave states, the door to the subconscious swings wide open, giving us a full view of what is running our lives from all those hidden places. As we cleanse ourselves of these negative emotions, many of the physical symptoms associated with the memory, the places where the subconscious has stored the emotions, also dissipate along with the feelings.

The American Institute of Stress reports that "75% to 90% of visits to primary care physicians result from stress-related disorders" (Leaf, 2008, p. 9). That's an astounding statistic: Stress causes up to 90% of all our diseases! In being "fearfully and wonderfully made" (Ps. 139:14), the design of our bodies includes this mysterious link between our intellect and emotion. It's a profound link indeed that impacts our physical as well as emotional health, especially as a result of emotions buried deep in our subconscious, which can wreak havoc. Emotions buried in the subconscious control nearly everything. With EFT, however, these emotions can be rooted out, discharged, and of no further consequence to our health.

Because the subconscious is literal, it often makes me shake my head at what physical symptoms are associated with particular emotions. For example, one of my clients had an outbreak of what he called "carbuncles." After the third one appeared, I suggested that he tap and get to the root emotional cause.

After a couple tapping sessions that centered around multiple different emotions he felt regarding his divorce of 20 years ago, I realized what better place for a divorce-based "carbuncle" than on his genitals—divorce, sex, gonads! But even more amazing was the fact that the genital "carbuncle" oozed for days. The client's word for the oozing was "weeped." Again, what an appropriate word to use when discussing divorce emotions! His body was "crying" over the divorce! These "carbuncle" outbreaks all occurred within 2 months. It has now been over 2 years since his EFT sessions and the client has not had any further outbreaks of "carbuncles."

The subconscious is truly amazing. And even more amazing, this literal physical-emotional connection is something we EFT practitioners see all the time.

Brad's Story: An Angry Boil

In another instance of skin eruption, a boil-like thing once developed on the back of my husband's neck. Though I asked Brad to tap on it, he did nothing at the time. The boil turned into a nasty infection, necessitating an antibiotic and continuous use of a heating pad for days. He missed several recreational activities because of the "infection."

Another "boil" appeared about 5 weeks later, but this one disappeared on its own. Lo and behold, a third one showed up 3 inches from the original one, this time on his shoulder. All I said to him was, "Here you go again. If I were you, I would be tapping on this right now!" At that, he plopped down in a chair and asked me to help him.

My only regret is I didn't videotape this session. I wish I had taken a picture of the "boil" before we began tapping. The session was classic Clinical EFT in its textbook form. His emotional body was crying out for help. It had now repeated its request for the third time, manifesting physically, hoping Brad would listen to what it wanted and needed. Let me illustrate why.

We began tapping. I asked what emotion he felt about this "boil" and he indicated it was fear, with a SUD score of 8. He tapped it to 0. In some ways, this session was an experiment. Obviously, I would never do this with a client, but while Brad tapped, I kept working my nighttime routine. In other words, I just led him through the process, but my attention wasn't fully present with him. EFT is so very forgiving, though, and the way I operated during this session undoubtedly proves that EFT has little to do with the practitioner! We simply serve as a guide and facilitate the process — God does the healing!

As soon as he tapped his fear to 0, I asked what he was now feeling. "I don't know. This came up so suddenly, I have no idea what to think!"

Good enough for this practitioner! "Oh," I said, "sounds like shock and surprise to me."

Brad agreed and rated the "shock and surprise" at 9 on the SUD scale.

I gave him the same instructions I had with his fear. "Tap it down and let me know when you are finished," I told him, and kept on with my work.

When he achieved his 0 SUD level, I asked what he now felt. Brad couldn't come up with anything, so I asked him to go back into his memory to the first "shock and surprise" in his life. Immediately, he said, "When the doctor told me I had to have my tonsils out!" We've encountered this relatively "nasty" childhood doctor before in our tapping, so I knew how he felt about that man. His SUD level was again an 8. "Dr. LeGree had no empathy for anyone, even children," Brad told me. He had tapped on several crude remarks this doctor made to him and about him to Brad's parents regarding his posture. Brad's scoliosis was never diagnosed or taken into consideration by this doctor.

"Tap it down and let me know when you are done," I instructed him, as I went on with my chores.

We continued this process for another two episodes. His next "shock and surprise" memory was his pilonidal cyst surgery while in the navy. That memory had a 7 SUD level attached to it. He tapped it away.

Let me interject here that the Holy Spirit gave me the intuition to know exactly where we were going in this process, but it wasn't my session, so I bit my tongue, not permitting myself to get ahead of him. It was Brad's session, so all the information had to come out of his mouth, not mine. I had mentioned to my husband on several occasions in the previous 6 months that there was an incident in his life that I knew, without a doubt, he needed to clear when he was ready. And I was right on, because here it came.

The SUD rating on the pilonidal cyst incident went to 0, but when I asked him his next "shock and surprise" event, out popped the statement, "When my ex-wife told me she was leaving me." Aha! There it was! His divorce of 25 years ago, plain as day, and now out in the open for his tapping attention!

By this time, I had finished my chores, and we were comfortably seated in our family room with me now giving Brad my full wife-practitioner attention. Let me tell you, this is where videotaping would have been wonderful.

I surely wasn't going to miss this timely opportunity to clear my husband of his divorce-related emotions. Brad classically went through about 12 different emotions, each ranging 7 and 9 on the SUD scale, tapping each down in succession, as Clinical EFT instructs, only to have the next emotion show up right on the heels of the one ahead of it. He uncovered discouragement, hopelessness (marriage counseling), anger, confusion, helplessness, shame (there were a couple of different aspects to this emotion), humiliation, disgust, and more.

He cleared the dozen or so emotions around the divorce, and he did so fairly rapidly. There was little discussion about why he felt what he felt. It was approaching 10:00 p.m. by this point, close to bedtime, so I told him he was getting the "Sherrie Smith Speed Tapping" method. He laughed and we tapped simply and directly on what emotion came up for him, with no embellishments. We tapped on "Anger, anger, anger," for example, at each acupressure point—nothing else.

Brad surprised me during this session with the number of new and different emotions he brought to the surface, as he usually only comes up with three emotions around his divorce—anger, frustration, and sadness. His personal tapping is mostly centered around these primary three. As we experienced tappers know, however, that is good enough, as long as the person tunes in to the physical sensations and/or the feelings themselves. The body knows exactly what is going on and will clear itself without the need for any fancy words or statements.

EFT in its simple purity worked to perfection! After a 75-minute tapping session, centering mostly around Brad's feelings about the marriage ending, I had him test to be as sure as possible that we had cleared his body and asked him to "look" into that "boil" again to see if it had anything else to say that night. He did so, and assured me there was nothing else at the present time. I wasn't convinced that a 75-minute tapping period had completely cleared the lingering weight of a painful divorce, but his body would let us know if more work was needed in the future.

Some added fun details of the rest of this story: Within 15 minutes of the end of this session, I looked at

Brad's "boil" and couldn't believe my eyes! Over 50% of the 2-inch reddened area around the "boil" had diminished, leaving a slightly pink area in its wake. I knew in my heart of hearts that the "boil" would be nearly gone by morning and shared with him this intuition of mine. He said he felt "light" after the session and agreed that his shoulder would look different the next day.

He kept a heating pad on his shoulder during the night. With the previous "boil," he had used the heating pad for 12 days plus taken a 10-day course of the antibiotic cephalexin, but the "boil" was still festering and angry-looking (red) for another week thereafter.

The following morning, with unbridled enthusiasm, I could hardly wait to see what his shoulder wound looked like. And God didn't let me down—75% of the "boil" had dissipated overnight! 75%! The 2-inch area of redness around it that had turned pink the previous night had now returned to his natural skin color. The "boil" had shrunk about 3/4 in size and was beginning to dry up. I'm thrilled to report that within 2 days of tapping on the issue of his divorce, the "boil" was completely dried up, scabbed over, leaving only a 10% remnant of its original self from 4 days previously. As a nurse, I know a boil of this sort would normally require antibiotics in order to clear.

EFT had worked its God-given healing again. God's EFT and a heating pad provided a miracle right before our very eyes.

Ellen's Story: Post-Stroke Symptoms

Here is another case that clearly illustrates the body-mind connection.

I've known Ellen for a decade or so. As sisters in Christ, we have shared much of what life has given us, and sometimes what we wish our Lord would take away, too.

Honestly, it took me a long time before I ever brought up to Ellen that I had embraced EFT. I simply assumed she would be another one who would have reservations about it. I later realized my hesitancy was unfounded.

Ellen has had a few oddball diagnoses, ones that even I as a nurse had never heard of. Because of these medical problems of hers, she was on a boatload of medications. At one time, she was taking 10 or 12 different prescriptions a day, some of which compounded her problems by interacting with the other meds, with side effects begetting more side effects. Some of the medications were potent to the point of interfering with her daily life, but she felt she had to take them because her migraine headaches in particular would pop up more frequently without them. Her migraines were debilitating in and of themselves.

A couple years ago, Ellen suffered a stroke, which compounded her problems. At first, she appeared to have no residual side effects from the stroke, but within a year, it became quite apparent that she had a huge memory deficit. Eventually, she was forced to retire from her high-pressure job.

She had been unemployed for about a year when EFT entered the picture. When she finally called me for tapping, she said, "God has healed me of all my emotional issues, so I don't know what exactly we will tap about, but I'm willing to try it anyway."

We opened the session with prayer. In this case, I asked Ellen to pray, rather than for me to do it. I then asked which of her symptoms was bothering her the most at this moment. As she tapped, the answer came to her, "My left eye is blurry. It discourages me because I can't do what I want, nor can I study my Bible. I just can't see clearly enough. It's a leftover effect from the stroke, I guess."

I asked what in her life wasn't clear to her.

Ellen tapped for about 30 seconds and said, "Did you know John had an affair about 15 years ago? I told you that, didn't I?"

She had indeed told me and I had suspected that this painful incident was still buried emotionally. It didn't surprise me that it had come up.

"So tell me the story about the affair," I said.

She began explaining in detail, tapping all the while, how she figured it all out, how she confronted John about it, and how hurt she was. "I walked out that night and went to a friend's house, staying there most of the night, talking to her."

When I asked how she felt besides "hurt," she answered, "Betrayed, lonely, it was all so private, and I didn't feel I could talk to many people about it, but I so wanted to talk about it. It really tore me apart, that betrayal. I didn't want to gossip about John, but I was so hurt, so I just cried out to my God in the midst of all that pain."

For not having anything to tap about, Ellen had gone right to the heart of the matter. She was sobbing now, so I didn't need to ask about the SUD level. She tapped and cried, cried and tapped, on all the betrayal and loneliness of that hurtful episode.

Somehow, through it all, she forgave John and their marriage was saved. She praised God for that miracle, as her children were still young at the time. The SUD score on betrayal and loneliness dropped to a 1.

We still had time left to tap, so I asked her what else was bothering her vision, causing the blurring in her left eye.

Suddenly, a SUD level of 6 popped up around her relationship with her mom. "Of the siblings, I'm the last one she asks about, nor does she ever ask about my kids or John. Her focus is always on all the rest of them. I do all the work for her, but they all get the credit. My sister drives by Mom's house and never stops. My brother has stripped Dad's workshop of all the good tools. John does woodworking, too—doesn't anyone think we might like some of the good stuff too? Mom mistreated Dad. He always had on dirty, spotted clothing. Mom mistreated me, too."

Ellen began to cry again, so for a minute or two we tapped in silence, allowing all that she had said to settle down a bit before we proceeded.

No emotions were identified with this eye-blurring aspect. I just let her continue to talk, telling me everything she had wanted to get off her chest for a very long time.

Ellen continued, "Mom was a bear in menopause. Dad never said anything, but I knew what she did to him. I saw it all." She indicated this memory was at a 4 on the SUD scale; the first one had been a 6.

"I was never good enough for her. She always told me how smart the rest of them were, but I guess she didn't think I was very smart. I did all the studying; other kids goofed off in school. I always had high test scores, and I still do, even after this stroke. No one ever told me the sky was the limit. Mom never saw any potential in me at all. I was the compliant one, and Mom never appreciated me. Now I fear I'm turning into my mother." That fear had a SUD rating of 3.

I now decided to do my tapping and prayer with Ellen, so we began:

Lord, I'm so sorry I feel this way. I know I have great potential because You made me.

I feel terrible complaining about all of this, Lord, because my life really isn't all that bad, even though sometimes I am discouraged about it, especially these physical issues.

Please forgive me, Lord, for the anger and bitterness I hold in my heart.

I know You sent Jesus to the Cross for these sins, and that You have removed them as far as the east is from the west from Your memory.

Lord, You've forgotten them because I confessed them, so why can't I forget them?

Why do I still harbor this bitterness in my heart? I want to let it go.

Please take away this anger at my mom so I can live in peace with her.

All this bitterness and anger, Lord, I give it to You now.

At that point, I asked Ellen to close her eyes, and visualize with me the following scene: "Picture Jesus hanging on that Cross right in front of you. See Him there, hands and feet bleeding because of the nails those soldiers hammered into them. See the blood dripping from His hands. Picture His mother, Mary, and John, the favorite disciple, standing right there beside you. Now look up into Jesus' dying eyes, and listen carefully to His words, 'It is finished.' Remember, He died on that horrible Cross over 2000 years ago for these sins of bitterness and anger, and anything else associated with them. Listen to His words again, 'It is finished,' and pull them into your heart right now. Make them part of who you are right now. *It is finished.* Your sins are forgiven."

Ellen had cried through much of this session, but she now sniffled a bit, and said, "I do feel better. Yes, Jesus did die for all my sins. I'm forgiven. Why does any of this other stuff really matter?"

We ended the session with prayer.

A month later, I phoned Ellen to see how she felt, and asked if she wanted to tap again. She said she was busy right then, but she had been to the brain doctor for a checkup and the doctor discontinued four of her medications because he didn't feel she needed them anymore. She was back to doing her Bible study, and never mentioned the blurry vision again. I asked if she thought the tapping had anything to do with that, but she didn't really think so.

This is a good example of what is called the Apex Effect, in which a client doesn't give EFT credit for any of the results that seem obvious to the practitioner. It is always interesting when EFT is never mentioned following a healing. Often the emotional charge, or even the event itself, disappears from the memory. The client might forget there was even a problem. In the end, however, what really matters is that God used EFT and me to help Ellen get better. It gives me great joy to serve the Body of Christ!

A year later, Ellen and I did another session. I learned later that Ellen is down to only three medications total out of the multitude she had been taking for the past decade — Praise God!

That's the beauty of Christians utilizing EFT. Body, soul, and spirit can now be fully integrated. As 3 John 1:2 says, "I pray that you may enjoy good health and that all may go well with you, even as your soul is getting along well." This reconnection is one of the many beauties that Christians will discover using EFT.

8

Using EFT to Cope with
Negative Emotions

We humans have two primary emotions: love and fear. They can't coexist. When we are feeling love, we can't feel fear, and vice versa. It is physiologically impossible. Under the umbrella of fear are its many variations—anxiety, envy, doubt, frustration, and anger. Satan is happy when we are in fear, as fear keeps us separated from God!

Even with the gift of prayer, we are still human, and our thoughts can readily lead us to worry, fear, discouragement, and anger. As we go through each day, prayer should be our first response to everything that makes us fearful, anxious, or angry. Those negative emotions keep us dependent upon ourselves and our own abilities and thoughts, instead of depending upon God's grace, mercy, and help. Unceasing prayer is the humbling of ourselves through continual dependence upon and communication with our heavenly Father.

God gave us prayer and God has now also provided us with Emotional Freedom Techniques as an effective tool for eliminating our negative patterned responses once and for all. Though He allows worry, fear, and anxiety to be part of our human experience. These were added to the doubt that Eve had and were a by-product of our first parents, Adam and Eve, in the Garden of Eden. He has also given us a mechanism to relieve those emotions through tapping.

Catherine's Story: Extreme Anxiety and Worry

Catherine's son was about to be discharged from the military for medical reasons, having a bad back and cardiac problems. It had also become clear during his last leave that he was suffering from posttraumatic stress disorder (PTSD). Catherine was terribly worried about him.

As she sat in my office, her stoicism was evident. I could see her trying desperately to hold herself together. She pulled a package of tissues out of her purse, so I made sure I gave her permission to cry all she wanted.

I need not relate all the details of Catherine's story. I used the standard Clinical EFT short-form tapping procedure with her. In the beginning, Catherine talked without stopping to take a breath. She had to tell me the entire saga of her son's military career and how he ended up in the physical mess he was in. I couldn't get a word in edgewise. After about 5 minutes, I told her I would listen, but she needed to pick a tapping spot and just tap while she talked, using the tap and rant technique.

Everything had a SUD level of 9. Her son had been a star athlete in high school, but he had injured his back in basic training and something else went wrong with his heart, giving him a cardiac issue and impacting his health to the point the army forbid him to exercise. It took a governmental official to get the army moving on issuing her son's medical discharge, which was coming up soon. This meant he would soon be back home living with his parents again.

Her empty nest was about to be refilled and Catherine was scared to death! On his last leave, her son had slept with a loaded gun under his bed and had terrible nightmares, screaming out much of the night. "I'm scared for him," said Catherine, and her tears began in earnest.

To be honest, I have not had a client cry this long or sob this hard ever. Usually, the tears dry up within a few minutes, but not so with Catherine. She cried for nearly an hour. Some of the time, I simply sat next to her, saying nothing, except reminding her to continue to tap and telling her the pain would release (I hate to admit it, but I wasn't sure myself that it would, as I witnessed the depth of her despair).

Finally, the Holy Spirit gave me an intuitive hit that she was fearful that her son might commit suicide, so I said, "I'm afraid he will kill himself." The Holy Spirit surely had that one correct, as her sobbing started all over again. Then the core issue revealed itself. "I want all my kids in heaven with me. If he kills himself, I will never see him again." And her sobbing continued unabated. I told her that I pushed the issue, saying what the Holy Spirit whispered to me. It was the most awful truth she was actually thinking—the bottom line for her, so to speak. The unspeakable had been spoken. Negative emotions cannot stand up any longer under tapping. God used EFT to shine His light and truth into her personal darkness.

With the core issue now out in the open and her tears finally subsiding, Catherine and I finished up on a few other emotions, including sorrow, regret, anger, and feeling stuck.

When Catherine left, I could see clarity in her eyes and a steadiness that hadn't been apparent when she'd arrived, and I told her so. She had nicely reframed most of the issues on her own by the end of the session and I could see she was now ready to take them on, however they presented themselves. We tapped on a few of her favorite Bible passages to seal the deal. I had her lead us with her favorite Scripture passages, which included:

"The Lord speaks to me and guides me in my every step." (Isa. 28:11)

"I trust in the Lord with all my heart and lean not on my own understanding." (Prov. 3:5)

"God will meet all my needs through the glorious riches that are in Christ Jesus." (Phil. 4:19)

"I seek first in all things His Kingdom and His righteousness." (Matt. 6:33)

"I fix my eyes on Jesus, the author and finisher of my faith." (Heb. 2:2)

We repeated each verse about three times. Catherine and I both needed to hear these words from God, as

Scripture is an excellent reminder of Who is always in control, especially as she anticipated her son's return home.

EFT excels at cutting through stress and worry, taking us back to a state of relaxation, allowing us to short-circuit the fight-flight-freeze (FFF) survival mechanism implanted in us (see Chapter 2). The neural networks are reconfigured. We unlearn the cognitive patterns of our earlier years, breaking down those destructive habits (like Catherine's worry) that keep us locked in a stressful state, whatever the origin.

Note: EFT has provided breakthrough treatment for returning soldiers and others suffering from PTSD. EFTUniverse.com founder, Dawson Church, PhD, has been on the forefront in researching as well as teaching EFT for this specific use. Read the *New York Times* article "A Revolutionary Approach to Treating PTSD" (Interlandi, 2014) and learn more at www.Stress Project.org.

Mary's Story: Fearfulness and Feeling Stuck

Mary sought my help in tapping on her resistance to her "new life." Retirement loomed and she wanted to create a different stream of income to supplement her savings. "I've tried many things, but nothing has panned out for me," Mary said. As she talked, I told her to begin tapping on an acupressure point of her choice.

Mary actually went on for quite some time, explaining her background to me. She was a fairly new client, so we were still getting to know each other. Though it could appear to outsiders that I wasn't doing much to help her by allowing her just to talk, I knew that if Mary tapped while she was talking, it would work just as well as a structured session. She was releasing all the angst around the childhood memories she was relaying to me.

Mary finally said, "I feel stuck." It was now time to tap in earnest. I inquired as to where she felt the "stuck" sensation physically and what emotion was attached to it. "Embarrassment and it's in my chest. It's affecting my breathing," she replied.

"Keep tapping," I said, "and go back in your mind and tell me the first time you felt embarrassment in your chest."

About 15 seconds later, the event revealed itself. "My kindergarten teacher brought me to the front of the room and put me on her lap," Mary recalled. "I was embarrassed by the attention."

"What is your SUD level around the embarrassment?" I asked. "It's a 10!" was her reply.

We tapped on the embarrassment of being in front of the class and the being "stuck on the teacher's lap."

Within a short time, Mary's SUD level dropped to 5. I asked my usual question, "How come it is isn't a 0?"

Mary's answer was interesting. "I don't recall struggling. I was passive and accepting in the teacher's comfortable soft lap. I felt love, but I was embarrassed by it all." She went on to share that apparently from an early age she realized her family's financial struggle. She always told herself a high school class ring "didn't matter," when in reality it did. She never got one. "My oldest sister was out there and always got what she wanted. I never spoke up for myself. I was the 'goody two shoes,' according to my sister." Mary went on, "I remember being given a bag of used clothing that fit me. I ironed them up to wear to school the next week and my sister took them and wore them instead. I let her do it." There were a few other incidents around babysitting and the high school prom that entered into her memories and subsequent tapping.

I inquired as to what emotion all this elicited. "Sadness and regret," Mary said, and gave them a SUD level of 4.

We continued tapping on the three emotions and bits and pieces of the events for a short time. It all quickly vaporized to a 0 on the SUD scale.

Mary was thrilled. As always, I was amazed how "stuck" in kindergarten manifested years later as "I feel stuck." Mary said, "I've tapped on this many times, but I never made that connection. That was an immense help to me. I can't wait to see where all this goes as I step out into my new life!"

Just as Mary felt "stuck," the rest of us can feel stuck in life, too. In times past, someone told us we weren't able or shouldn't do one activity or another. Those adults injected some "limiting belief" into our impressionable minds. We then simply stopped trying new ideas or activities for fear we really couldn't do them or worry that we would look foolish to those around us.

EFT is the great lubricant for moving those negative memories out! It "unsticks" us and then initiates positive thoughts we never thought possible.

I, too, can't wait to see where this all leads for Mary. EFT is a wonderful tool for exploring and rooting out the early embedded beliefs we have about ourselves and who we think we are. The limits we put on ourselves as a result of these beliefs have no basis in reality. We can be anyone or do anything we choose, no matter our age, once we uncover and dismantle the blockage we unconsciously succumbed to early in life.

Roberta's Story: Chronic Family Issues

Roberta is a long-term client with whom I have tapped about a dozen times. These are the cases that are fun to watch and clients that are rewarding to work with because they are actively committed to changing their lives for the better. The old life that wasn't working well for them has to go, ushering in a new way of living that is much healthier as well as peaceful.

Within the next month, Roberta's adult daughter and her three grandchildren would be moving in with her, due to the daughter's circumstances, an idea that had arisen 2 months before. Roberta related to me as she started to tap, "I'm letting go of my daughter and allowing her to do her own stuff. She just doesn't hook me anymore. I've set down the ground rules for moving in and she is open to them all, for the first time ever. I'm really excited for this to happen, as it will give me some quality time with my grandchildren."

It is encouraging for me to see how Roberta's entire attitude has changed over the past 7 months we have been tapping. Her daughter used to trigger her emotionally over everything, both small and large incidents. It appears that all of that has changed with the immense amount of tapping work Roberta has done. Her diligence in utilizing EFT and working through these problematic patterns are now paying big dividends for her.

In this session, we did some mopping up. Roberta was still feeling a bit of dismissiveness from her daughter that was "living" in her chest with her usual "halting breathing," as she described it. Roberta went on, saying, "I'm cut off when I talk and am not being heard, like I have nothing to contribute. It all makes me feel worthless."

We tapped through those feelings, and then I asked her to feel into her chest and tell me another incident from her childhood days that matched the feeling. Roberta and I have tapped on a lot of her childhood incidents, and, as always, they related perfectly to what she was feeling today, and how she handles her life now.

"My older sister, Veronica, was a screamer and yelled to get her point across. I allowed myself to stay on the sidelines and not be seen. My mom was like that too—the strong silent type. I have no idea how anything was ever resolved in that household. I guess things just petered out on their own," Roberta said.

We tapped through that dismissiveness and unworthiness, with her reporting her chest was less tight, and her breathing easier.

When I asked what else was happening, up popped "resentment." She continued, "I'm not going to tolerate stuff from my daughter when she lives here. We've been doing this dance forever and it now has to stop. I need to make sure the ground rules are perfectly clear."

We tapped out the resentment, which wasn't overly high on the SUD scale, at a 4.

Earlier Roberta had mentioned being "concerned about what other people think," so we went back to that thought. She felt that in her chest, too, at a SUD level of 5. "People give me all kinds of advice, but they never fix their own stuff. I still gauge a bit of my worth and well-being around what others say," Roberta told me. She had no particular emotion associated with this, so we simply stayed with the physical feeling in her chest and tapped.

I then asked her "to feel into that chest tightness" and pull out an early childhood incident for me. Roberta and I have tapped for so long that she knows exactly what I'm looking for and exactly why I'm doing the looking. She understands that these early childhood incidents set the stage for how we view life in adulthood. We pattern ourselves today based on the patterns we learned as children. Our neurochemistry is all the same, today as yesterday. It becomes a matter of internal habit for us.

"Dad pops up," she says, "but I don't have an incident exactly. I remember him being there, but doing nothing in life. Oh, he was helpful with homework and gardening, but I feel a negative field around him." She did report her chest suddenly became much tighter again, and so we began to tap. Roberta was obviously having a physiological reaction to something in her memory if her chest was reacting in this signaling way.

We tapped four of the acupuncture points, then she spoke, "I resented him for calling me and asking me for money in order to make the younger kids' Christmas nicer. I had just graduated, gotten an apartment and a car, and I didn't have any spare cash. Why was he doing nothing and expecting me to support the family? I really resented that."

The resentment was at about 7 on the scale, so we surely had something to tap on here. "Resentment, resentment, resentment" is how we worked, and I tossed in a couple of comments about what her dad said, using her exact words.

It all broke fairly quickly, and Roberta reported she felt really good, and her chest had released, with her breathing much easier.

The appointment time was nearly up, but I went back over a few points we had tapped on, inquiring if it was all gone now by having her again feel into her chest and check on all of it.

There was a wee bit of something left in her chest. With a tiny bit of tapping, she reported it as "anger." Apparently, her daughter assumes that what is Roberta's also belongs to her. She relayed to me a recent cookie incident. We tapped the anger out of the cookie incident.

I did tell Roberta that I could hear the difference in her voice compared to the last time we tapped. Something had shifted, something had changed. Her tapping work is clearly paying off well for her.

Roberta is a not a Christian, but she does describe herself as "spiritual." Just before we tapped this session, she spent about 10 minutes explaining to me how her "spiritual" practice has changed over the past 2 months. Though I wish Roberta was a sister in Christ, I understood what she was explaining to me. Whether we are Christian or not, EFT opens up something deep inside us that yearns for a connection to our Creator. Obviously, EFT can't make you into a Christian, but I believe God just allows whatever He created within us to do whatever it does from our personal worldview. We Christians simply receive a deeper connection to our God because of the teachings of our faith and, most important, our relationship with Him.

Annette's Story:
Abortion Regret and Sexual Immorality

This case study illustrates how God used EFT to free a sister in Christ of guilt following an abortion 30 years earlier. She had confessed the abortion as sin "a hundred times," but she didn't feel the emotional release from it that she so desired until we applied the healing balm of EFT.

Annette indicated she had a fairly high anxiety and stress level around the impending death of her father who was gravely ill. Her SUD score was a 7.

Prior to tapping, I began our session with this prayer: "Holy Spirit, please sit here with us today. Bring to mind anything we need to know to clear this anxiety for

Annette. Whisper in both our ears what we need to know to lead her through this process in order to give this precious child of Yours the peace she so desires. Holy Spirit, you are my 'intuition' because You created us all and You know us intimately, inside and out. You alone will receive all the glory and honor for what You are about to do for us. We pray this in Jesus, our Savior's name, amen."

Setup:

Even though I have all this stress because I know Dad is going to die soon, I know God loves me.

Even though my anxiety level is through the roof, I know Jesus loves me.

Even though I'm already worrying about how I'm going to handle all the hassles of the estate with my brothers and sisters after Dad passes, I know God loves me very much.

TH: *I can't stand all this stress about Dad.*

EB: *I'm nearly beside myself worrying about all the stuff I will have to handle.*

SE: *I know the other kids are going to give me all kinds of grief about the house.*

BE: *I can't live here forever; the house is too big.*

UL: *I won't have anywhere to go when Dad dies.*

CH: *I can't imagine how I will be able to handle all this.*

CB: *All this work that is going to fall on me when Dad dies, so I try to keep him alive as long as possible.*

UA: *Dad's dying and I can deal with that because he's old; it's all the after stuff that's so hard to think about.*

We did a couple rounds of tapping around these issues, with Annette changing a few words here and there to match what she was feeling. At that point, I stopped her and had her drink some water, breathe deeply, and tell me where her SUD level was now and what she was thinking.

Her SUD level had come down to a 3 or 4, but a new aspect had arisen. "I talked to Jimmy [her husband] about this, but I think I deserve all this hassle and shouldn't be complaining at all about it because I had that abortion in high school." Annette went on and on for a good 15 minutes about this issue, so I let her talk, but I told her to keep tapping while she "ranted." Her SUD score had gone back up to a 6.

We tapped:

TH: *I deserve all this hassle.*

EB: *It's all my own fault that I have to deal with this.*

SE: *I know God has forgiven me, but I still feel guilty.*

UE: *When I don't feel guilty, I feel guilty because I don't feel guilty, and I think I should be feeling guilty.*

UL: *I worry about what other people are thinking. They think I should have more remorse than I'm showing.*

CH: *How can I face that child in heaven? I killed that baby.*

CB: *I deserve what I get taking care of Dad. I caused it all.*

UA: *This is my punishment for what I did. Someone has to pay for killing that baby.*

Annette was crying pretty heavily about the abortion, but under the tapping, it soon slowed. We stopped after two rounds, reevaluated, drank some water, and retested. Her SUD score was down to a 2.

Annette indicated another aspect had popped up. "I have no self-control with food. I have all these weight issues, which are punishment, too, for what I did." Hesitantly, she went on about her lack of interest in sexual matters, saying, "My body is tired and not holding up well." She was frustrated with herself, "doctors, insurance, and hospitals." Now that the subject of sexuality had opened up, she discussed for a short time the Catholic Church's teachings in this area. I just allowed her to talk, heard only by me, without prejudice or comment.

Her SUD level went back up to a 10. No Setup needed. We went right back to tapping.

TH: *I'm disgusted with myself.*

EB: *I have no self-control. I just keep stuffing food in my mouth.*

SE: *I've gained all this weight and I can't keep up in life.*

UE: *I've lost all interest in sex and Jimmy just keeps going.*

UL: *I'm just so tired keeping up with Dad and the kids.*

CH: *I'm frustrated with myself that I can't seem to be able to do this job.*

CB: *I'm tired of all the doctors, insurance, and hospitals. They wear me out too.*

UA: *I'm so very disgusted with myself, but I know God still loves me.*

After three rounds with reminder phrases and statements along these lines, we again stopped for some deep breaths, a drink of water, and to check where she was—still at a SUD score of 7.

Because this was a phone session, I was listening intently for any changes in her voice. I knew she was starting to break down, as her voice began cracking, and realized she was now near tears. I asked how she was. Annette told me this all brought back an incident from when she was 12. During one of the previous breaks, I had quickly explained to her that EFT was particularly effective if one could link the present emotion to a childhood event. Annette had just come up with a childhood event.

I told her to keep tapping, which she did while she told me this story. While playing hide and seek around an old building with some friends, a man ran up to her and grabbed her across her chest, on "my boobs," then ran off. None of her friends witnessed it, but she told them about it when they returned. Her girlfriends asked why she hadn't screamed. "I tried, but nothing came out" was her answer. Of course, none of them believed her, so one of her friends asked, "Did you enjoy it?" Her answer was an emphatic no, but she realized she had a bit of sexual arousal around the event, so in came the guilt and conflict over not being able to scream and the "nice" feelings.

"I was a coward for not standing up for myself. I was too weak to scream. I was too weak to say no to the abortion. I was too scared to make a decision about anything. And now I can't make any decisions about much of anything either." This all came streaming out of her without a break.

I asked for a SUD rating, which I suspected was pretty high because the tears were really beginning to flow. Again, no Setup was needed, as she was definitely in the moment, her SUD level was an 8, and she was in tune with her intense feelings. I asked if she had tissues left. She did. I could hear her blowing her nose—a lot!

TH: *I'm a coward.*

EB: *I don't know how to stand up for myself.*

SE: *I was too weak to say no to the abortion.*

UE: *I'm too scared to make any decisions about anything.*

UL: *I tried to scream. Nothing came out.*

CH: *I'm such a coward.*

CB: *I'm weak.*

UA: *I don't know how to stand up for myself.*

Her crying had slowed a bit, so we continued.

TH: *I was alone when that man came.*

EB: *I told my girlfriends what had happened.*

SE: *They asked why I didn't scream.*

UE: *I did scream, but nothing came out of my mouth.*

UL: *He grabbed my boobs.*

CH: *I was so surprised and embarrassed.*

CB: *Did you enjoy it?*

UA: *Did you enjoy it?*

Her crying began again, so I continued. I knew I was hitting a really sore spot with Annette and I wanted to disarm it quickly and thoroughly.

TH: *Did you enjoy it?*

EB: *I couldn't scream.*

SE: *He grabbed my boobs.*

UE: *Did you enjoy it?*

UL: *No one believed me. He ran off.*

CH: *I feel guilty because it aroused me.*

CB: *I feel that guilt, but I know God has forgiven me.*

UA: *God forgave me, as I was only 12 and it wasn't my fault. I didn't ask for it.*

Her crying slowed again, but I did another round on the hand points on the final four statements to make sure the issue was gone.

We reevaluated again, along with getting another glass of water for both of us, and taking some deep breaths. Annette said she felt much better and had a SUD score of 2.

Another aspect change showed up as Annette's voice softened and I knew she was thinking about something else now.

"That progression of growing up with so much immorality. All that femininity. I allowed guys to walk all over me. I was so promiscuous. I never told Jimmy too much about it because I feared it would damage our relationship. He said he didn't want to know. I was taught right and wrong. I feel so guilty. I remember feeling like trash. I was always heavy and bigger than my older sisters, but everyone told me I wasn't heavy. I was just big boned. I was told I looked like Dad, and Dad always had weight issues until recently, so I figured I would be fat too." After a pause, she spoke again, "What am I going to say to that baby when we meet in heaven?"

I assured her that the baby was in heaven and I suspected the child would run to Annette, wrap her arms around her, and say, "Hi, Mom!" I asked Annette if she had confessed her sin to Jesus. "A hundred times, but I still feel so guilty," she answered. I had her tapping while she talked.

Usually, I ask a client where they physically feel such issues, but Annette had no problem articulating what she was feeling, nor did she have any problems getting into the moment with these issues. She was such an easy client to work with even though this was all being done over the phone. She was once again beginning to cry. I asked her to give me two different SUD levels—one on the "immorality" and another on the weight issue. Both were at 10.

I decided to do one at a time, rather than confuse the issues. This would enable me to know where the SUD level was on two different topics and ensure I disarmed both of them adequately. To approach them separately rather than together was simply my choice as a practitioner; there is no right or wrong here.

We began again without a Setup, as she was sniffling quite a bit, with me tapping using her own words:

TH: *All that growing up.*

EB: *So much immorality.*

SE: *I allowed guys to walk all over me.*

UE: *I never told Jimmy much of this.*

UL: *I felt like trash.*

CH: *I'm ashamed of myself. How can God put up with me?*

CB: *I went to all those clubs and drank like a fish night after night.*

UA: *All this guilt over that behavior.*

The next round continued, with her crying subsiding, although not completely:

TH: *All this immorality.*

EB: *I didn't feel too feminine, so I let the men walk all over me.*

SE: *Those men used me and I let them.*

UE: *I knew right from wrong. I was taught better than this.*

UL: *I feel so guilty.*

CH: *If I tell Jimmy, it might damage my marriage.*

CB: *I felt like trash.*

UA: *I still feel like trash.*

Her crying was now nearly finished, so I went one more round:

TH: *I feel like trash and I killed that baby, but I know God loves me.*

EB: *I feel so ashamed, but I know Jesus died on the Cross for me and this shame.*

SE: *I feel so guilty because I killed my baby, but I know Jesus loves me very much.*

UE: *I let men use me because I wouldn't stand up for myself, like I didn't stand up for myself when I was 12.*

UL: *I think I can let myself forgive me because God loves me and forgives me.*

CH: *I think I can forgive myself because Jesus forgives me.*

CB: *I do forgive myself.*

UA: *I do forgive myself because Jesus has forgiven me and has tossed those sins as far as the east is from the west.*

Annette was down to a SUD level of 2 on the sexual immorality guilt and shame. She wanted to leave just a little to remind herself of how she had behaved in her younger years and to keep from ever taking for granted all the forgiveness God and other people have given her on these issues. That was her choice and I honored that, as I knew that the SUD levels of both could well drop lower when the calm and peace of the EFT effects set in.

We next tackled the SUD 10 issue of weight:

TH: *I was bigger than my older sisters by the time I was 8.*

EB: *I'm not heavy. Everyone told me I'm big-boned.*

SE: *I'm so ashamed of my size.*

UE: *I look like Dad and he always had weight issues.*

UL: *I figured I would always be fat like Dad since I looked like him.*

CH: *I was bigger than Sis and that made me feel fat.*

CB: *I think I can forgive myself for my weight.*

UA: *I know I can forgive myself for my weight.*

We did a second round on this with that round emphasizing the forgiveness part a bit more. This weight issue dropped like a rock to a big fat 0 (pun intended)!

Annette was elated by how wonderfully relieved she felt and wanted to leave the session right there. She commented on the Christian aspect of forgiveness and "how much God does love me," to which she said, "I needed to hear that, so thank you." I gave her instructions to keep tapping daily but not neglect her prayers, confess her sins daily, and particularly make sure to go over her day with the kids mentally and tap away any problems or issues to prevent them from building up into a larger emotional burden.

It was a classic EFT session, Christian style. I checked on Annette via e-mail the next day. She was thrilled because "I feel so calm today and I don't know why!" I giggled and told her, "It's the EFT. That's the way it works! God gave you a miracle."

Another text arrived from Annette some time later thanking me again for taking time to tap with her. "I've never had this much peace in my life. Many of my fears and anxieties are gone. I've lived with those for years. God is so good. I'm grateful He sent me to you. I'm sorry Bill (my brother) died, but what a benefit to me that he did as I then reconnected with you."

Since then, I have followed up with her routinely and the peace that God gave Annette through EFT has not diminished. God is indeed faithful to us!

Anne's Story: Anger and Fear of the Future

While tapping through some childhood issues, Anne happened to mention that she had recently visited her doctor for her yearly physical exam. The doctor reviewed her family history, as he does every couple of years. She had told the doctor before that her mother had died of breast cancer a few years prior to her dad dying from a massive heart attack. This time she mentioned that not only had her father died of a heart attack, but so had all four of her father's brothers. The doctor nearly went ballistic over this supposedly new piece of genetic information. "Why didn't you tell me this before?" Dr. James asked Anne. "You never asked me what my aunts and uncles died from," she replied.

"This is too much heart history to ignore," said the doctor. "We better do some more tests on you just to make sure you aren't in the early stages of something, too." The doctor concluded, "You'll probably die of a heart attack before any cancer gets you."

I asked Anne how she felt about what the doctor told her. Her answer is pretty typical of most of us, "I guess I better watch it. The doctor should know. It's his profession, after all."

"Would you like to try some tapping on this issue before we continue with the rest of our session?" I asked.

"Yes, we'd better," she replied. I instructed her to close her eyes, pick any tapping spot she wanted, think about the doctor's words, "You will probably die of a heart attack," and tell me if she felt anything anywhere in her body.

Anne tapped for a short time, opened her eyes, looked at me, and said, "Yes, I do feel something, and it's in my chest, right over my heart." I asked her to describe it for me.

"It feels like a tight, gripping, pinching pain, like something is constricted in my chest," she said. "It's not bad, and I probably wouldn't have noticed it had you not asked me to think about it. That's odd."

"How do you feel now about the doctor's words? Give me an emotion."

"I feel really sad and fearful. I almost want to cry thinking about what he said to me," she answered. I asked if she felt the sadness in her chest, too. "Yes, I do, and now it's pinching even more than before," Anne said.

When I asked her to rate the SUD level of the sadness, she closed her eyes, assessing the feeling, and answered that it was 8.

We began tapping:

All this sadness and fear about dying of a heart attack.

The doctor said it was a good possibility.

He should know, he's the doctor, not me.

Mom died of cancer, but he says a heart attack will get me.

All this sadness. It's like some psychic telling me.

I guess it is all generational and genetic.

I'm doomed to it, it's a done deal. A heart attack will get me.

The doctor said so. He must be right. It's his job to know.

We tapped three rounds with similar words and ideas around the doctor predicting a fatal heart attack. When we stopped, I asked Anne what her SUD level was around the sadness now. It was 3.

When I asked what else she was feeling, she said, "I'm really mad now. How dare he say that? What does he know anyway? He's not God." She rated the feeling at a SUD level of 9. "He really ticks me off."

We tapped again:

> *He makes me so mad.*
>
> *What does he know anyway? He's not God.*
>
> *I'm so mad.*
>
> *I'm furiously mad.*
>
> *How does he know that?*
>
> *He's not God!*
>
> *I'm so darn angry. He's got nerve saying that to me.*
>
> *I'm so mad.*

Two rounds of tapping on "mad" brought that SUD score down to a 2.

"You once told me we could tap on generational things. Is the heart attack one of those?" Anne inquired.

"I would surely think so," I answered.

"Let's tap on that," she requested.

We tapped:

> *All this generational stuff. I reject it all.*
>
> *Only God knows when and what I will die of. No doctor can predict that.*

Jesus took all those bodily curses onto Himself at Calvary. No doctor can change that!

My body will function as God created it to.

My genetics are directed by God, my Creator, not by some doctor.

I reject it all. No generational genetics are going to take me.

God is my Savior and my Creator and my Sustainer. Nothing any doctor says has any hold on me, unless God so ordains it.

Jesus is my healer and protector. I reject all this generational stuff.

At that point, I inquired how her chest felt. "It's all gone!" she exclaimed. "No pinching or grabbing or anything. It's all gone. That doctor doesn't have a clue. No heart attack is going to take me. I have so much work yet to do for God's Kingdom. I simply have no time to waste on this fear."

One more time, just to retest, I asked Anne to feel into her chest, and ask if there was anything left around the notion of heart attacks.

"No, nothing left," she said after a moment. "In fact, I think I can hear my heart purring. I know that sounds funny, but it's a comforting feeling. I like it. Let's go back to what we were doing. I'm done with this issue. Thanks for thinking of it for me!"

Anne's case serves as a reminder to check whether what you hear has a negative impact on you, either emotionally or physiologically, before you dismiss the words as meaningless. This doesn't mean you must think about every word spoken to you in the course of a given day, but do so for words that come from some authoritative source and then tap if there is a negative impact. The reason negative criticism given to children tends to stick with them for the remainder of their lives is that it comes from a higher authority—a parent, guardian, teacher, or older sibling. The subconscious grabs it and makes it our very own truth, which, in the end, tends to become our reality, whether good or bad.

Clearing the Way to God

Stormie Omartian, a popular contemporary Christian writer, says, "Once you have taken that first step, God will show you other steps to take. He will teach you how to walk in the light of His truth, revelation, and love. You'll discover ways to avoid the things that separated you from Him and enjoy all He has for you. You'll learn to walk away from fear, depression, condemned loneliness, loss, unforgiveness, and disappointment" (Omartian, 1999, p. 169).

All of these emotions Stormie lists are feelings that EFT deals with well. Although doing EFT may still seem a little scary to you, maybe today will be the time to step out and make the first move for yourself, your family, and your friends.

"He will teach us His ways and we shall walk in His paths." Micah 4:2b.

"If the Lord delights in a man's way, He makes his steps firm." Psalm 37:23.

Afterword: EFT's Transformative Power Can Change Our World

With EFT, we have a new opportunity to impact our hurting world in bringing the Christian ideals of love, compassion, and forgiveness into direct action in our relationship with ourselves and each other. With EFT, we can clear the way to be the Christians we have hoped, prayed, and ultimately aspired to be—free of the emotional burdens that have kept us from living our lives as fully as God intended.

Together, let's change the general MO of societal rules, like Jesus and the Apostles did in their era. Did you know that many of the major economic and religious movements that shaped world history were started by only a handful of men? For example, communism, as we knew it until 1984, began with less than a dozen followers of Lenin right after the Russian Revolution of 1917. Mohammed had his few followers. Jesus had His 12. And EFT research shows the same type of trajectory potential. I hope my statistic is close here, but it takes something like less than 1/10th of 1% of any given population to change the "energy" or behavior of an entire region.

We Christians are a huge force for good in our world, if we would only apply ourselves to generating that change, as Jesus instructed us to do: "Therefore go and make disciples of all nations, baptizing them in the name of the Father and of the Son and of the Holy Spirit, and teaching them to obey everything I have commanded you. And surely I am with you always, to the very end of the age" (Matt. 28:19–20).

Changing the world includes a life of obedience to the will of God and listening to the voice of the Holy Spirit, often walking a very narrow path, diligent in our honesty, integrity, and morality, enabling us to live life for Jesus, and having a positive influence on those around us. The world should not change us; we must instead be changing the world for Christ. We need to ask for "the mind of Christ" (1 Cor. 2:16b). And we are now blessed to discover God has given us some amazing physiological and emotional resources in EFT, with its unique ability to clear harmful memories and limiting beliefs plus powerfully minister to their hurtful physical manifestations, which ultimately enhances our relationship with Him and others. So it's time we marshal our forces and begin using this new resource in earnest. The time has arrived. We may all have been called for such a moment as this. Casual Christianity is out; "Energy Christianity" is in. The Christian EFT "revolution" has begun!

So it is my ardent hope and prayer that you, dear reader, will embrace this tool of healing. And as it unleashes its transformative power in your life, then teach these concepts to your children, as well as share your reports with your friends and fellow Christians for EFT's possible implementation in their lives. If each of us makes a small effort, teaches others to do the same, and shares the necessary instruction, we can watch the world change before our very eyes within a decade or two.

A deep concern of mine is that many, perhaps most, pastors and priests don't have sufficient time in their day to advise or to talk with their hurting congregational or parish members. As a result, many people simply slip through the church's cracks. Understaffed churches simply cannot meet the needs of all their members. Consider the possibility of Christian EFT practitioners picking up this slack for the pastors or priests. This is a viable option, especially monetarily. A congregation could have a certified and insured Christian EFT practitioner either on staff or on referral, depending on what arrangement best suited their needs and resources. As a result of my own EFT practice, I'm convinced that most problems church members face can be repaired with the application of EFT. Surely, it's time to give EFT a try. The investment needed is minimal, but the results for God's Kingdom could be enormous. I pray all church hierarchies will consider hiring certified, insured EFT practitioners.

Let's take the world for Christ, making it a wholesome, healthy place to dwell until Jesus comes back to take us all home to heaven.

Jason Gray sums it all up well in this uplifting excerpt from his song, *With Every Act of Love:*

With every act of love
We bring the Kingdom come
God put a million, million doors in the world
For his love to walk through
One of those doors is you.

God really does have a million doors for love to walk through, and EFT is just one of them. I pray you find your open door and you help to bring the Kingdom come!

My Story, in Closing

A simple morning stroll bore witness to that very verse and this theme of being mindful. Here is what happened one beautiful morning and how EFT can help us open up and find renewed peace.

My husband and I were in Rochelle, Illinois, on a short railroad vacation. Rochelle is a small, lazily quiet western Chicago prairie town sporting wide avenues, tall older trees, and quaint Victorian homes.

Walking down these wide tree-lined streets, I gazed upward through newly sprouted leaves to the blue sky beyond. Wisps of fluffy white clouds and jet trails from planes approaching O'Hare or Midway airports streamed across the sky. I spied a kitty hunkered down behind some gnarled tree roots, pretending to hide from the prey it was stalking. Gloriously colored spring flowers were everywhere—tulips ablaze, hyacinths blooming, and the ever-present yellow dandelion, popping up in all the lawns, some meticulously manicured, others in need of a good mowing. The wind was whispering through the trees, gently stirring the leaves. In the background, I could hear the laughter and calls of children at play. It was Memorial Day weekend and red, white, and blue flag buntings hung from second-story porch railings, reminding me of those pictures of the antebellum Lincoln-Douglas debates. I wondered if either of them had done any stump speeches in Rochelle. No detail escaped me — I saw it all. And I pondered the magnificence of it all too.

Details of God's wonderfully thought-out creation surrounded me. The beauty of small things is astounding in its intricacy and symmetry. How did He think up so many different ideas to place here on earth for all of us to enjoy?

All was well in my world, as I strolled along, listening to Steven Curtis Chapman sing "Glorious Unfolding" via my headset. "God is not done with you yet," Steven sang. I rejoiced in fully realizing I'm here right now, in the present. Awake, alive, completely enjoying all the sights and sounds around me, praising God for the millions of blessings He bounteously bestows on each of us. I had not a care in my mind at that moment. Although I had a hundred things to do when I got home, I was totally mindful of the present moment in time. I was fully there; all the chores and cares of the world had rightfully settled into the back of my mind.

In the moment is where I like to dwell nowadays. This is where I would like to teach others to dwell, if they are not there already. Being in the moment, in my mind, is what life is all about, the way God created us to be — totally at peace, inside and out.

From the corner of my eye, I glimpsed a police car about to pass from behind me, its lights flashing in silence. I realized the police car was leading a funeral procession. Someone had lost a loved one. The parade of cars was lengthy, all with their headlights ablaze, some with tiny purple funeral flags stationed on the roof of the car, and one or two with yellow flashing lights. Everyone was bound for the cemetery, a familiar sight in America. For a moment, nothing shattered my peace, but then I began to feel my physiological response.

Dwelling in the present, I was aware of every little change. My left scapula (shoulder blade) began to ache a little, then the left middle chest heart pain chimed in, a steady stabbing of sorts, harsh, asking to be heard, too. Soon thereafter, my eyes filled with tears. I fluttered my eyelids a few times, wishing them away. These feelings were as real as the azure sky and the odd smell of the creeping Charlie growing on the damp side of the old trees. For decades, I never paid attention to what these feelings wanted to tell me. Now, after thousands of hours of tapping, I do. It all means something. Everything has meaning.

I discern what my reaction to the funeral procession means for me. I miss my brother Bill, and I miss Grandma and Grandpa. Oh, how I miss them. To share this gloriously beautiful late spring day with them would be a prayer come true, but they are in heaven, seeing it from a vantage point that someday I, too, will enjoy. I no longer ignore the feelings. I embrace them. They are part of who I am and part of God's gracious plan for me. Slowly and gently, I begin tapping on my chest.

I tap not to forget the people I love, but to allow those feelings to move through me. I allow them to just release themselves. I know I need to tap whenever a memory pops up and is accompanied by a physiological response. I have no need for the physiological part of the memory — after all, that results in raising my cortisol level, my blood pressure, and my pulse rate, interrupting my peace, my tranquility, and my communion with God.

Only a few minutes of tapping are needed, as I acknowledge what I'm thinking and feeling, praying to my heavenly Father during this on-the-go EFT session. My tears dry up, shoulder pain and chest pain are released, and I smile.

EFT has done its job once again. What a momentous gift. Memories of Bill come flooding in. That's the beauty of EFT — as it pulls out the emotional impact of the accumulated grief, it leaves behind in its wake a wonderful blessing. Those muddy footprints of grief give way to mountains of positive memories of the loved one. The chest pain is replaced by a warm, loving feeling that wells up deep out of my heart for the brother I loved while he lived and the brother I still love while he dwells in heaven, having made it there ahead of me. Those memories seem more precious than ever to me. Through EFT, God has replaced grief with beautiful memories, bright, shining ones that simply make me smile.

Thank you, Father, you have given me a gift straight from heaven. This EFT is an invention of yours to heal us. You show us how to live each moment in the beauty of your earth as we await that which is surely more spectacular than our imagination can possibly fathom—heaven. I stand grateful forever in Your magnificence. Amen.

Many of us have prayed for years—maybe even for decades—that God would deliver us from one thing or another, be it a physical illness or an emotional problem. Often, we blamed God because He didn't seem to be listening. We would find some new technique or idea and think, "Ah, this is the answer," only to fall flat on our faces once again, reverting to the exact spot where we began. Eventually, despair or desperation set in. We all know about Saint Paul's "thorn in the flesh" (2 Cor. 12:7–10). He never explained precisely what it was, but it sounds similar to some of the problems and annoyances we grapple with today.

The Book of Joshua tells the story of the Israelites crossing the River Jordan on their way to the Promised Land after 40 years of wandering in the desert because of their unbelief in the God who saved them from the Egyptians. The Lord told Joshua that as soon as the priests' feet touched the water of the River Jordan, the river would part, allowing the Israelites to cross on dry land.

How many of you have wandered in the desert of your emotional and/or physical problems for what surely seems like 40 years, wondering when God was going to deliver you from their grip? God has sent you a tool to help you find your way out of the desert: EFT. I urge you to step out in faith and use this God-given tool.

I encourage you as a Christian to learn EFT. It's putting into action a powerful method to help and heal those who are in emotional pain. Let's step into this gap of a hurting world, standing up for those in emotional pain, tapping and praying with them, and allowing God to grant them health and wholeness. God will be so pleased to see us ministering to each other in this new and powerful way.

With EFT, you now have a way to help a friend or loved one who is having a particularly bad day and seems only able to cry or complain. Try tapping with them. While you tap, pray for your friend. Pray for healing and wholeness. Quietly pray or pray aloud, whatever feels comfortable. "Therefore confess your sins to each other and pray for one another so that you may be healed" (James 5:16). You have just *stood in the gap* for a friend because you prayed for that person's healing, helping them to clear negative emotions from the past that keep getting triggered by present encounters or circumstances.

We are told to do what we can in the natural world, allowing God to take care of the rest. Believe for friends that the Hand of God will touch them, until they can believe it for themselves. "Therefore I tell you, whatever you ask for in prayer, believe that you have received it and it will be yours" (Mark 11:24). For those of us who know EFT, God equips us and commissions us to move forward and minister to others. Saint Augustine said it best, "Without God, we cannot. Without us, God will not."

Jesus stood in the gap for us when He went to the Cross for us, absolving our sins. EFT is another example of Jesus' great compassion to those who are hurting. Right now it's the best tool out there, and the science has proven it. EFT is precisely what any Christian struggling with emotional or physical pain needs to learn to use, and then share with others.

Dear Christian brothers and sisters, please consider your life in light of this new science-based breakthrough. God has called us to health, light, and life. EFT will open up your spiritual life once you have taken the steps necessary to use this simple practice to eliminate the over-burdening thoughts, habits, and troublesome past events from your past that influence your present. Once God no longer has to push through your "junk," you can hear Him much more clearly. If you allow it to do so, EFT will create a dynamic and fulfilling new dimension in your Christian walk...and that's my sincere prayer for you.

For you created my inmost being; you knit me together in my mother's womb. I praise you because I am fearfully and wonderfully made; your works are wonderful, I know that full well.
(Ps. 139:13–14)

References

I have read or used these books for reference and informational purposes, but I do not advocate all of the ideas, thoughts, or processes promoted in them. All these books must be read utilizing the reader's discretion, based on God's Word.

Aron, E. N. (1996). *The highly sensitive person: How to thrive when the world overwhelms you.* New York, NY: Broadway Books.

Barr, S. M. (2003). *Modern physics and ancient faith.* Notre Dame, IN: University of Notre Dame Press.

Blackstone, J. (2012). *Belonging here: A guide for the spiritually sensitive person.* Boulder, CO: Sounds True.

Bonhoeffer, D. (1953). *The cost of discipleship.* London, UK: SCM Press.

Bonhoeffer, D. (1954). *Life together.* New York, NY: Harper & Row.

Braden, G. (2007). *The divine matrix: Bridging time, space, miracles, and belief.* Carlsbad, CA: Hay House.

Braden, G. (2008). *The spontaneous healing of belief: Shattering the paradigm of false limits.* Carlsbad, CA: Hay House.

Bubeck, M. (1975). *The adversary.* Chicago, IL: Moody Press.

Carrington, P. (2008). *Try it on everything: Discover the power of EFT.* Bethel, CT: Try It Productions.

Cherry, R. (1999). *Healing prayer: God's divine intervention in medicine, faith, and prayer.* Nashville, TN: Thomas Nelson.

Church, D. (2009). *The genie in your genes: Epigenetic medicine and the new biology of intention.* Santa Rosa, CA: Energy Psychology Press.

Church, D., Feinstein, D., Palmer-Hoffman, J., Stein, P. K., & Tranguch, A. (2014). Empirically supported psychological treatments: The challenge of evaluating clinical innovations. *Journal of Nervous and Mental Disease, 202*(10), 699–709.

Church, D., Yount, G., & Brooks, A. J. (2012). The effect of emotional freedom techniques on stress biochemistry: A randomized controlled trial. *Journal of Nervous and Mental Disease,* 200(10), 891–896. doi:10.1097/NMD.0b013e31826b9fc1

Clemons-Jones, K. (2012). *Cured but not healed: How to experience deeper faith on your journey with God.* Prospect, KY: Professional Woman Publishing.

Collinge, W. (1998). *Subtle energy: Awakening to the unseen forces in our lives.* New York, NY: Warner Books.

Dawson, K., & Allenby, S. (2010). *Matrix reimprinting using EFT: Rewrite your past, transform your future.* London, UK: Hay House.

Dean, H. B. (1987). *The golden treasury of bible wisdom.* Uhrichville, OH: Barbor Books.

Dispenza, J. (2007). *Evolve your brain: The science of changing your mind.* Deerfield Beach, FL: Health Communications.

Dossey, L. (2000). Prayer and medical science: A commentary on the prayer study by Harris et al and a response to critics. *Archives of Internal Medicine, 160*(12), 1735–1738.

Dunn, R. (1991). *Don't just stand there, pray something.* Nashville, TN: Thomas Nelson.

Eden, D. (2008). *Energy medicine: Balancing your body's energies for optimal health, joy, and vitality.* New York, NY: Jeremy P. Tarcher/Penquin.

Edes, G. (2011). Saltalamacchia says yips are gone: Red Sox catcher swears by his work with sports psychologists. *ESPN Boston,* February 9, 2011. Retrieved from http://sports.espn.go.com/boston/mlb/columns/story?id=6103972.

Fang, J., Jin, Z., Wang, Y., Li, K., Kong, J., Nixon, E. E.,... Hui, K. K.-S. (2009). The salient characteristics of the central effects of acupuncture needling: Limbic-paralimbic-neocortical network modulation. *Human Brain Mapping, 30,* 1196–1206. doi:10.1002/hbm.20583

Feinstein, D. (2012). Acupoint stimulation in treating psychological disorders: Evidence of efficacy. *Review of General Psychology,* 16(4), 364–380. doi:10.1037/a0028602

Feinstein, D. (with Eden, D.). (2011). *Ethics handbook for energy healing practitioners.* Fulton, CA: Energy Psychology Press.

Feinstein, D., Eden, D., & Craig, G. (2005). *The promise of energy psychology: Revolutionary tools for dramatic personal change.* New York, NY: Jeremy P. Tarcher/Penguin.

Felitti, V. J., Anda, R. F., Nordenberg, D., Williamson, D. F., Spitz, A. M., Edwards, V., Koss, M. P., & Marks, J. S. (1998, May). Relationship of childhood abuse and household dysfunction to many of the leading causes of death in adults. The Adverse Childhood Experiences (ACE) Study. *American Journal of Preventive Medicine, 14*(4), 245–258.

Flook, R. (2013). *Why am I sick? How to find out what's really wrong using advanced clearing energetics.* Carlsbad, CA: Hay House.

Gallo, F. P., & Vincenzi, H. (2008). *Energy tapping: How to rapidly eliminate anxiety, depression, cravings, and more using energy psychology* (2nd ed.). Oakland, CA: New Harbinger.

Gibson, R. (2008). *My boy, my earth.* Bloomington, IN: iUniverse.

Graham, H. (2001). *Soul medicine: Restoring the spirit to healing.* Dublin, Ireland: Newleaf.

Greene, B. (2004). *The fabric of the cosmos: Space, time and the texture of reality.* New York, NY: Alfred A. Knopf.

Hayford, J. (2004). *The hidden power of praising God.* Eugene, OR: Harvest House.

Haynes, W. F., Jr., & Kelly, G. B. (2006). *Is there a god in health care? Toward a new spirituality of medicine.* New York, NY: Haworth Pastoral Press.

Holdway, A. (1995). *Kinesiology, muscle testing and energy balancing for health and well-being.* Rockport, MA: Element.

Hover-Kramer, D. (2011). *Creating healing relationships: Professional standards for energy therapy practitioners.* Santa Rosa, CA: Energy Psychology Press.

Hughes, S. (2000). *Discovering life's greatest purpose.* Nashville, TN: Broadway and Holman.

Hughes, S. (2003). *Every day with Jesus: The spirit-filled life.* Nashville, TN: Broadway and Holman.

Hughes, S. (2004). *Every day with Jesus: The armor of God.* Nashville, TN: Broadway and Holman.

Hui, K. K. S., Liu, J., Marina, O., Napadow, V., Haselgrove, C., Kwong, K. K.,…Makris, N. (2005). The integrated response of the human cerebro-cerebellar and limbic systems to acupuncture stimulation at ST 36 as evidenced by fMRI. *NeuroImage, 27,* 479–496.

Hunt, S. (2009). *Spiritual mothering: The Titus 2 model for women mentoring women.* Wheaton, IL: Crossway/Good News Publishers.

Interlandi, J. (2014). A revolutionary approach to treating PTSD. *New York Times Magazine,* May 22, 2014. Retrieved from http://www.nytimes.com/2014/05/25/magazine/a-revolutionary-approach-to-treating-ptsd.html?_r=0

Jeeves, M. A., & Berry, R. J. (1998). *Science, life, and Christian belief.* Grand Rapids, MI: Baker Books.

Johnson, H. (2008). *Tragic redemption: Healing the guilt and shame.* Austin, TX: Langmarc.

Koenig, H. G. (1999). *The healing power of faith: Science explores medicine's last great frontier.* New York, NY: Simon & Schuster.

Kuchinskas, S. (2009). *The chemistry of oxytocin: How the oxytocin response can help you find trust, intimacy, and love.* Oakland, CA: New Harbinger.

Leaf, C. (2008). *Who switched off my brain? Controlling toxic thoughts and emotions.* Dallas, TX: Switch on your Brain.

Lipton, B. (2008). *Spontaneous evolution: Our positive future (and a way to get there from here).* Carlsbad, CA: Hay House.

Luther, M. (1959). *The large catechism of Martin Luther.* Philadelphia, PA: Fortress Press.

Luther, M. (1986). *Luther's small catechism.* St. Loius, MO: Concordia.

MacNutt, F. (1977). *Healing.* New York, NY: Bantam.

MacNutt, F. (2006). *The healing reawakening: Reclaiming our lost inheritance.* New York, NY: Baker Books.

Matthew, V. (n.d.). *Faith affirmations.* Grand Rapids, MI: Grand Rapids Baptist Bible College.

McTaggart, L. (2003). *The field: The quest for the secret force of the universe.* New York, NY: Harper Collins.

Missler, C. (2012). A holographic universe? (Featured briefing). Koinonia House, Coeur d'Alene, ID. Retrieved from: http://www.khouse.org/articles/2012/1086

Missler, N., & Missler, C. (2000). *Be Ye Transformed.* Koinonia House: Coeur d'Alene, ID.

Moberg, K. U. (2003). *The oxytocin factor: Tapping the Hormone of Calm, Love, and Healing.* Cambridge, MA: Da Capo Press.

Morgan, R. J. (2001). *The Red Sea rules: 10 God-given strategies for difficult times.* Nashville, TN: Thomas Nelson.

Napadow, V., Kettner, N., Liu, J., Li, M., Kwong, K. K., Vangel, M.,...Hui, K. K. (2007). Hypothalamus and amygdala response to acupuncture stimuli in carpal tunnel syndrome. *Pain, 130*(3), 254–266.

Omartian, S. (1999). *Just enough light for the step I'm on.* Eugene, OR: Harvest House.

Ortner, N. (2013). *The tapping solution: A revolutionary system for stress-free living.* Carlsbad, CA: Hay House.

Pert, C. B. (1997). *Molecules of emotion: Why you feel the way you feel.* New York, NY: Scribner.

Pert, C. B. (2006). *Everything you need to know to feel go(o)d.* Carlsbad, CA: Hay House.

Roberts, M. D. (2005). *No holds barred: Wrestling with God in prayer.* Colorado Springs, CO: Waterbrook Press.

Russell, B. (2014). New book highlights success of clinical EFT tapping. Retrieved from http://www.examiner.com/article/new-book-highlights-success-of-clinical-eft-tapping

Scaer, R. C. (2001). *The body bears the burden: Trauma, disassociation, and disease.* New York, NY: Haworth Medical Press.

Shealy, N., & Church, D. (2006). *Soul medicine: Awakening your inner blueprint for adundant health and energy.* Santa Rosa, CA: Elite Books.

Sheldrake, R. (2003). *The sense of being stared at and other unexplained powers of the human mind.* New York, NY: Crown.

Sherrer, Q., & Garlock, R. (1991). *A Woman's guide to spiritual warfare: A woman's guide for battle.* Ann Arbor, MI: Servant Publishing.

Sibbes, R. (2000). *A Puritan golden treasury.* Carlisle, PA: Banner of Truth.

Washington, G. (2011). *Rules of civility and decent behavior.* Chestertown, MD: Literary House Press.

Yancey, P. (2006). *Prayer: Does it make any difference?* Grand Rapids, MI: Zondervan.

Bibles

The Amplified Bible, Lockman Foundation, 1958.

The Bible in Today's English, American Bible Society, 1976.

The English Standard Bible, Crossway (Good News Publishers), 2001.

The Good News Bible, American Bible Society, 1976.

The King James Bible, Thomas Nelson and Sons, original printing 1611.

The New American Bible, Thomas Nelson and Sons, 1971.

The New American Standard Bible, Lockman Foundation, 1975.

The New International Version Bible, American Bible Society, 1984.

New Living Translation, Tyndale House, 2007.

The New Revised Standard Version Bible, National Council of Churches, 1978.

EFT Resources

For information about EFT, including a free downloadable Get Started package, go to www.EFTUniverse.com. On this website, you'll find thousands of case histories of people who've used EFT successfully for every conceivable problem. You'll also find practitioner listings, tutorials, books, DVDs, classes, volunteer opportunities, and other resources to allow you to get the most from EFT.

If you want to learn more about Christian EFT for your personal use, are interested in becoming a Christian EFT practitioner, or would like to schedule an EFT class or seminar in your church or for your group or organization, contact the author:

Sherrie Rice Smith, RN (Ret), EFT-EXP
Mentor of Christian Women
Certified EFT Practitioner
EFTUniverse Trainer Levels 1 & 2
Matrix Reimprinting Practitioner
Ad Majorem Dei Gloriam

www.EFTforChristians.com

Index